THE MATURE STUDENT'S GUIDE
TO HIGHER EDUCATION

LINDA PRITCHARD WITH
LEILA ROBERTS

Open University Press

Open University Press
McGraw-Hill Education
McGraw-Hill House
Shoppenhangers Road
Maidenhead
Berkshire
England
SL6 2QL

email: enquiries@openup.co.uk
world wide web: www.openup.co.uk

and Two Penn Plaza, New York, NY 10121-2289, USA

First published 2006

A catalogue record of this book is available from the British Library

ISBN-10: 0 335 21773 7 (pb) 0 335 21774 5 (hb)
ISBN-13: 978 0335 21773 1 (pb) 978 0335 21774 8 (hb)

Library of Congress Cataloging-in-Publication Data
CIP data applied for

Typeset by YHT Ltd, London
Printed in Poland EU by OZGraf. S.A.
www.polskabook.pl

CONTENTS

ACKNOWLEDGEMENTS

The author would like to thank the following.

The students who provided advice and guidance so that other mature students could benefit from their experiences: Ros Burgess, Tony Carlton, Christine Cooke, Julian Debenham, Julie Goddard, Craig Lowe, Bernadette Oxbury, Glynis Rushby and Maureen Wilcox.

Melanie Smith for her very positive feedback on the text.

David Barr, Julie Goddard and Lis Johnstone for their continuous support.

Leila Roberts for being such a positive study skills tutor and fun to work with over the last few years.

All my family and friends for their support and encouragement.

INTRODUCTION

Go and do it. It is a life changing experience – and not as hard as you may think.

(History degree student)

Are you ready for a change in direction? Do you want to return to study and do a higher education degree? If so, this book is intended for people like you who would like to do a higher education degree course as a mature student.

You might be considering returning to study for a number of reasons. These might include seeking a change in your working life, returning to work after a break, having a need to retrain and learn new skills or refresh existing skills, or you may simply want to study for pleasure. Whatever your reasons, this book will help you prepare for your return to study.

Each chapter looks at issues relating to returning to study and to higher education and guides you through the decisions you need to make. You can use this book either by reading through the chapters in turn or by dipping into chapters at random – it depends on how much you already know about studying and higher education. If it is new to you it is advisable to start at the beginning of the book and work your way through each chapter in order. If you already have some knowledge use the contents list and index to find the most relevant parts of the book.

At the beginning of each chapter is an introduction which tells you what it relates to and what you should know when you finish reading that chapter. Some chapters make reference to information contained in other chapters and this allows you to cross-reference information when you need to.

Throughout the book there are references to real mature students' experiences and quotations from mature students. Speaking to a mature student is one of the best ways to find out what studying in higher education is really like. Most are happy to share their experiences and the students who have contributed to this book have done so to help you make informed decisions.

Each chapter contains practical advice and guidance, as well as checklists to help you make decisions and references to organizations which provide advice for mature students.

Throughout the book there will be references to going to university. This is for ease of reference as higher education degrees are offered in a wide range of institutions, such as universities, colleges of higher education and colleges of further education.

The book begins by outlining why people study and why they return to education. You will be asked to consider your own reasons for returning and to reflect on your current skills and how you will be able to use them while you study. You will then find out more about barriers and how they might prevent people from returning to education. Once you identify your own barriers you can start to think about ways in which you can overcome them.

Chapter 3 covers preparation for study and outlines the skills required to do a degree course. The fourth chapter on study skills outlines some of the skills needed to succeed as a higher education student. There are other books containing more detailed guidance about study skills and it is always a good idea to buy a recommended study skills guide. You will find some listed at the end of this book.

Preparation and planning are the key to successful decision making and Chapter 5 explains what higher education is and describes the different ways in which you can study and the different ways degree courses are taught. There is also information about how to choose a university and a course and what you should consider when making your decisions (Chapter 7).

Finance is a common cause of concern for all students whatever their age and Chapter 6 looks at student finance. There are frequent changes in the financial support available for higher education students so, although this chapter provides guidance, it is wise to seek further advice at the time you are doing your planning and preparation. Contact details for organizations able to provide financial advice are listed at the end of the book.

Chapter 8 is about specific courses designed to help you prepare for a degree and advice on how to choose the most suitable one for you. This chapter also covers how to make a successful application for your chosen degree course.

Further chapters provide advice about getting ready for the start of your first term and guidance on how to keep motivated to the end of your degree course. A range of student support services are outlined so you know where to look for any help you need while you study.

Chapter 11 outlines career planning while you study and provides information on how to find the right job when you finish your degree course. Finally, there is a section on how to get further advice, with contact details of organizations referred to throughout the book, and a recommended reading list and bibliography.

Returning to education may seem daunting, but it is supposed to be a positive, enjoyable experience. If you plan and prepare well in advance there is a greater likelihood of your experience in higher education being a good one. Enjoy it and make the most of it.

Summary

This book will enable you to:

- use information and advice to help you return to study and acquire new skills;
- reflect on your motivation and desire to study;
- increase your understanding of higher education and make decisions about course choice and type of study;
- become aware of the range of skills required to help you study at higher education level;
- gain a realistic expectation about higher education before you begin your degree course;
- have a clear understanding of aspects such as student support and student finance;
- be thoroughly prepared for higher education by careful planning and preparation;
- make a smooth transition to higher education and enjoy your experience;
- understand the importance of career planning.

1

WHY STUDY?

This chapter will help you:

- identify what has motivated you to return to study;
- reflect on your existing skills;
- explore the benefits of returning to study;
- understand what learning means.

The three years I spent as a student were the best of my life.
(English literature and women's studies degree graduate)

Introduction

This chapter: looks at why you want to return to study; will ask you to reflect on your current skills; looks at some of the benefits of returning to study; and finally will examine what learning means.

It is important to look at your motivations to study before you start making decisions about the course you want to do and where you want to do it. If you know why you are motivated to make change you are better able to meet the challenge and manage that change in a positive way.

If you are currently studying you have probably already thought about your motivation to do so and the benefits of studying. You will probably also have reflected on your skills and managed your transition back into education.

Personal values

What is important to you and why? Each of us has a set of values, perhaps gained from our family, our background and our upbringing, and we find different things acceptable or unacceptable. Reflect on your values, why you hold them and how they might affect decision making about your future. This will help you understand what is motivating you to study and should ensure you make the right decision.

Motivation to study

Motivation can be described as an ambition or desire to do something. We should rarely do something without having a good reason to do so and ideally should explore and understand our reasons. Be clear about your motivating factors and keep referring to them while you study. Remind yourself why you are studying and what goal you have in mind.

> Why did I do a degree? A mixture of it being a challenge and to prove to others that I was capable of getting a degree.
> (English literature degree graduate)

You may identify with some of the following reasons often mentioned by mature students as providing motivation to study.

Many adults did not have the opportunity to study earlier on, particularly at degree level. They may have left school at 16, or earlier, with a handful of qualifications or no qualifications. They may have been under pressure to get a job at an early age or might have had families to support. Conventional attitudes to employment may have influenced their choice of job and prevented them from following their preferred path. Sometimes it is only later on in life that the opportunity to study presents itself.

Many mature students identify personal challenge as a great motivating factor in their decision to change direction and return to study. The challenge of undertaking a degree course and gaining a qualification can provide a significant boost for anyone who has previously been lacking in self-confidence. Proving something to yourself and others is often cited as providing motivation to study.

I have always wanted to gain a degree but feel the conditioning of my working-class background held me back. I decided to attempt a degree to challenge myself and to kick against my background, to prove to myself (and the world) what I am capable of.

(Foundation degree in rehabilitation student)

Some people choose to study because of circumstances such as redundancy or returning to work after a break from employment. This is a time for self-reflection and, although the circumstances can be daunting, it is the right time to make decisions about your future. In this situation you need to ask yourself if you want to continue with what you know and use your existing skills or whether you want to learn new skills and do something different. You might find your skills, however good they may be, are no longer required because of changes in the nature of employment and this means you face a need to retrain.

Some jobs require specific qualifications at specific levels. You need a degree to be a teacher, doctor, lawyer, physiotherapist, librarian, engineer, architect or a nurse. If you have a particular job in mind you may need to follow a particular training route to get there. Chapter 8 describes routes to higher education in more detail.

Lifelong learning means just that. Retirement from full-time work may provide an opportunity to study and, for some people, the first opportunity to study since leaving school. The concept of lifelong learning makes it more acceptable for people to return to study at any age.

Better pay and a desire for promotion at work may be your motivating factors. You may not want to change direction completely, but build on your existing skills and take them further. Classroom assistants may want to train as teachers, library assistants may want to train as librarians and occupational therapy assistants may want to become occupational therapists. Your working environment remains the same, but you gain a qualification which provides a career path within that environment. Be realistic about your career opportunities and speak to your manager or work colleagues to find out more about how you can improve your chances of promotion.

Learning for pleasure should not be ignored as an important motivating factor. You may not want promotion, a change of direction or to prove anything to anybody. You might simply want to learn something new. If this is the case you are in an enviable position. Your choice of course need not be limited to one that provides a good possibility of employment at the end of the course (an important consideration for many people). You can indulge yourself by applying for any course attracting your interest and can (within reason) dip in and out of study as you please, at your convenience. Of course, all learning, whatever your reasons for doing so, should be enjoyable.

Studying makes you think (or should do) and for many adults this is a good enough motivating factor. Routine jobs, perhaps done over many years, can dull the mind. Studying opens up new ideas and higher education promotes critical and creative thinking. If you are unfulfilled in your current job then studying may give you the challenge you need.

You may be motivated by an interest in a subject. This sounds obvious and all students should be interested in the subject they are studying. However, this is sadly not always the case and it is very difficult to keep up the momentum of study if the subject you are studying bores you. Remember this when you start to make decisions about your choice of course. Chapter 7 provides information about how to choose the right course for you.

A common motivating factor for mature students is that you may simply have reached a turning point in your life and this has prompted you to assess your current situation. This might have been triggered by a bereavement, divorce, illness, children growing up and leaving home or even a midlife crisis. The negativity of such events can be risen above by a positive reaction to change and a plan to improve your life.

You may have no idea what is motivating you to study, but have a real desire to do so. If this is the case then trust your instincts, take advice, be realistic and make what you feel is the right decision for you.

Many mature students are studying because of a combination of motivating factors and many factors are linked together. A lack of confidence earlier may have resulted in a limited opportunity to study. This may have meant employment in a routine job which has become boring and for which you are not well rewarded. Job satisfaction may be low and your desire to change may be motivated by your need for personal challenge, to improve self-confidence, your job prospects, pay and job satisfaction.

Use the following checklist to help you identify what your motivating factors are and prioritize these so you understand which are most important to you.

What are your motivating factors?	Tick which apply to you
Did not have the opportunity earlier on	
The need for personal challenge	
Want to boost self-confidence	
Made redundant	
Returning to work after a break	
Need to acquire new skills	
Bored in current job	
Need a particular qualification to do a particular job	
Just retired and got spare time	
Learning for leisure	
Want to get promotion at work	
You want to think	
Interest in a particular subject	
Turning point in life	
Other reasons	

Dealing with change

Most of us are creatures of habit. We may choose to go against the flow at sometime in our lives, but as we get older we tend to resist change. This is partly because our circumstances (mortgage, family, need for employment) prevent us exploring options for change or even considering change as an option for us. Despite this every day many adults are returning to study motivated by the reasons mentioned earlier on.

As you work your way through this book you will be asked to reflect on issues which might affect your decision making and ultimately affect how you change your life. Careful planning and consideration of all these issues will ensure you are better equipped to deal with your planned change and your planned degree course.

It is important not to rush into making a decision, but to take each step slowly. Many degree courses start in Autumn and you may have been advised to apply early to ensure you obtain a place. It is sometimes better to wait and plan than to rush into an application without careful consideration. Many degree courses are three years long and it makes sense to plan before entering into this commitment.

There is more about dealing with change and how change can affect you and other people in Chapter 2.

Self-reflection

Self-reflection helps determine where you are now and what skills you have and where you want to be and what skills you will need. You can then find out the most appropriate way to obtain these skills.

A lack of self-confidence means that adults sometimes underestimate their skills and do not recognize the skills they use every day, either at work or at home. Therefore, many mature students return to study without realizing they already possess useful skills for their new challenge. Studying will be a new experience for you; you will need to learn new skills to help you succeed and gain a qualification, but you probably already have a set of skills you can use too.

What have you done so far?

Reflect on five experiences you have had in your life so far. You could choose a particular job, having a child, moving house, going to school, getting married, an emergency, caring for someone, a particular day you remember, an achievement, a happy time, a sad time, leaving home, learning something new, or an argument. Look at the following questions and relate them to the experiences you have chosen.

- Have your experiences been varied, interesting, challenging, upsetting, enlightening?
- How did they make you feel?
- What personal resources did you use in each experience?
- What specific skills did you use in each experience?
- How did you cope with the experiences?
- Did your experiences change you in any way?
- Have you changed the way you do things because of these experiences?

Most experiences are useful, even those that are also painful, sad or challenging, as they encourage you to be resourceful and responsive. Even if you feel you have not dealt with some experiences in the best way this provides a lesson for how you do things in the future. Effective learning requires reflection and using experience.

There is more about how to assess your skills in Chapter 3.

Benefits of study

> I gained far more from higher education than I had anticipated. My self-esteem and confidence grew and I made good friends, friendships which are still continuing 12 years on.
>
> (English literature degree graduate)

You should now have a better idea of your motivating factors for studying. But what are the real benefits of studying and what benefits do people gain from their studies?

Learning new skills

Learning a new skill is an achievement in itself, but has practical benefits as new skills may help you get the job you want in the future. You might learn how to market a business on a Management Studies degree, how children acquire language skills on a Linguistics degree, or how to do sports massage on a Sports Studies degree. These new skills may be relevant to a particular job or open the door to a range of jobs of interest to you.

When you study you also develop 'soft' skills such as problem solving, communication skills, working in a group, questioning skills, negotiation skills and thinking creatively and critically. Soft skills are not as easily measured as practical skills, but are ones you need to use in everyday life, in your community and with your family as well as in the workplace.

Getting a job

Some courses prepare you for and are a requirement of that particular job. All new skills enhance your job prospects. Research has shown a link between low levels of qualifications and a high likelihood of unemployment and 14 per cent of people without qualifications are unemployed, compared with only 7 per cent of people with higher level qualifications. From an employer's point of view well trained and well educated staff can enhance productivity.

Personal and intellectual development

Obtaining new skills and achieving a qualification help personal and intellectual development. You will constantly surprise yourself by how you rise to the challenge of studying. You will probably be encouraged to reflect on this throughout your degree course and prepare a graduate profile of your achievements and experience.

A sense of achievement

A positive experience of learning provides a sense of achievement in something well done. Anyone with a previous negative experience of education will benefit from a positive experience later on in life and will probably be encouraged to continue studying.

Increase in confidence and self-esteem

Successful study, learning new skills and the sense of achievement this provides should help to increase your confidence and self-esteem. As you progress through your studies your self-confidence increases and you may find yourself achieving things which you would not have considered doing at an earlier stage in your life. If you take on a challenge and do well you feel better about yourself and more confident about your next challenge.

Better pay

Research has shown that, when it comes to earnings potential, all types of qualifications at all levels are better than no qualifications. It is wise to be realistic about this and if better pay is your primary or only motivating factor make sure you do some careful planning first. Having a higher-level qualification, such as a degree, can improve your chances of obtaining a well-paid job, but it is not quite as simple as it seems. There may be national shortages in some professions, (teaching and healthcare for example), but investigate the job situation in your area and try to obtain a local picture, particularly if you intend to stay in that area when you have finished your studies. Get some local advice about careers, be realistic and you should not be disappointed.

Increased job satisfaction

Anyone who feels stuck in a job with little or no job satisfaction would welcome moving to a job offering more job satisfaction. A qualification can open doors to a range of jobs and these might prove more challenging. As you gain in confidence during your studies the idea of taking on a job with increased responsibility becomes a more realistic possibility.

Health and well-being

Learning is good for the mind and the body. It makes you think, promotes an active life and enhances your physical and mental well-being. Studying can prevent isolation and encourages people to socialize.

New horizons

Studying opens up your world. Not only do you find out about the subject you are studying, but you also find out more about yourself, about other people and how they live and what they think. You may even have the opportunity to spend some of your study time abroad as many degree courses encourage this type of experience.

Meeting new people

There will be many social activities organized in colleges and universities and you may not be able to attend all of them. However, while you study you will meet a range of different people from varying backgrounds and some of them will remain your friends for life. The personal challenge of studying brings people together and encourages people to support each other.

Sharing your experiences

Even if you feel you have little background knowledge of your subject of interest you may have some life or work experience relating to it. Your fellow students will benefit from your experiences as you will benefit from theirs. Everyone has something of value to contribute and all students gain from sharing their experiences.

As you can see there are many benefits to be gained from study, but always be realistic. You may be looking for a total life change and your studies may not be the way by which you achieve this.

What does learning mean?

Learning should involve the following:

- taking in new experiences, ideas and concepts;
- linking ideas logically in a sequence so they make sense;
- connecting your learning to past experiences so that it makes sense and puts it in a context which helps increase your understanding;
- using creativity, imagination and visualization;
- being critical by asking questions and not making assumptions;
- making use of, and improving, your memory;
- learning by mistakes by reflecting on them and understanding why they happened;
- using reasoning skills;
- reflecting on your learning as you progress;
- building a bigger picture of your learning;
- demonstrating your learning.

Learning styles

People learn in different ways and there are a variety of ways of learning and a range of different learning styles. Previous experience may have introduced you to different learning styles, some of which you might have enjoyed more than others.

For example:

- Some people may enjoy listening to a lecturer speak while others may find it hard to concentrate when someone is speaking for a length of time.

- Some people may enjoy learning a skill by practical work rather than reading about that skill.
- Some people may enjoy group discussion and debate while others may find this daunting.
- Some students may prefer thinking about abstract concepts but others may prefer to take a more practical approach.

If you have used a limited range of learning styles in the past you may not yet have found your preferred way of learning. This can affect your experience and influence your feelings about how much you will enjoy learning in the future. It may also make you less confident about trying out different ways of learning.

Spend time thinking about two experiences of learning, one of which you enjoyed and one you did not. Think about what these experiences involved, for example listening, practical work, reading, group work. Consider why you liked one experience and not the other. For the learning you did not enjoy think about ways in which it could have been a better learning experience than it was.

The psychologists Honey and Mumford devised a questionnaire to help people identify what kind of learner they are and identified four different learning styles:

Activists enjoy new experiences and like to learn by doing and trying out. They welcome diversity, challenge and working with people. They enjoy more practical approaches to learning such as project work, field trips, brainstorming and discussion groups, but do not enjoy theory-based learning such as lectures, repetition, analysis, being passive and not being involved.

Pragmatists like new ideas and putting theory into practice and prefer a practical approach and techniques which help deal with particular issues. They enjoy learning which links theory into actual situations, such as a course with a work-based learning element. Pragmatists do not enjoy learning if there is no immediate benefit or reward and they find abstract ideas and concepts difficult.

Theorists need to understand theories and finer detail before taking action. They work methodically and like to question and analyse complex issues. Theorists enjoy research and reading and gaining information from lectures, but do not enjoy learning involving feelings and emotions and they find unstructured approaches difficult.

Reflectors think carefully, watch people and take a back seat to enable them to gain a wider view of a topic. They enjoy research, information gathering and processing. They also enjoy observations so would like learning which involves watching others. Reflectors take time to learn so may need flexibility to learn at a pace suitable to them. They do not enjoy learning which involves them leading or presenting and do not enjoy role play.

Some people will identify with one particular style, while others will be a mix of the four different learning styles outlined above. It helps if you can incorporate elements of all of them into your learning and become a flexible learner who responds to different learning environments.

If you are doing a degree course you will encounter a range of learning styles. Recognize your preferred learning styles, the ones you enjoy and are good at. Be open to new ways of learning and try out new learning styles. This will help you get the most out of your learning.

There are many books available about learning styles and some are listed in the section on Recommended Reading.

What next?

You have spent some time thinking about your motivation to study and why studying is important to you. You have briefly considered the importance of managing change and the importance of self-reflection and have read about the benefits of learning. Finally, you have reflected on what learning means and on your own learning and preferred learning styles.

The next step is to explore how you can overcome any barriers preventing your return to study and any anxieties you feel about returning to study.

2

BARRIERS TO STUDY AND HOW TO OVERCOME THEM

This chapter will help you:

- identify any barriers preventing you from returning to study;
- understand how to manage change;
- understand how to manage your return to study;
- find ways of dealing with any anxieties you have about returning to study.

With my starting college relatively late in life as a mature student, questioning my ability, or even the right to be there, was playing on my mind from the first day of the first term.

(Design and technology degree student)

Introduction

Many mature students say they wish they had studied earlier on in life and not waited until later to take up their degree course. They may previously have faced barriers, such as lack of time or money, which prevented them from studying. This chapter looks at some of these barriers and ways in which they can be overcome. It is possible that a combination of these barriers prevented you from studying earlier on. It helps to identify what these barriers are as this can help you overcome them now if you face them again.

This chapter will also help you reflect on how to manage change associated with returning to study and how to deal with any anxieties you have.

If you are currently studying you have probably already overcome some of your own personal barriers, managed change and dealt with some of your anxieties.

What are the barriers?

Limited opportunity to study

Many mature students simply did not have the opportunity to study beyond the age of 16. Some may have left school earlier. There may have been pressure to leave school and get a job to help out with family finances, or there may not have been a tradition in the family to go into higher education or to continue education beyond the age of 16. There seems to be a greater expectation these days that school leavers will go into higher education or at least continue in education after age 16 and now 42 per cent of 18- to 30-year-olds go on to higher education compared with around 5 per cent in 1960. In the past many people went straight into employment at age 16 and some then gained promotion by putting in time with the same employer.

Previous experience of education

For some people schools days were not the happiest days of their lives and these people are likely to have few fond memories of that time. This could be for all sorts of reasons such as bullying, family problems, lack of confidence or a fear of failing academically. All of these affect an individual's experience of education and can make people wary of returning to study in case the earlier experience is repeated. This is why it is important to make sure you take advice and get support if you wish to do a degree. Make sure you are on the right course, in the right place and have a realistic idea of what is expected of you. The fewer surprises the better and the more positive your new experience of studying will be. You will find higher education to be a very different experience from your school days.

It's not for me

Your experience at school might have reinforced stereotypes as to the type of subjects you were expected to study or the type of job you would get once you left school. Despite some changes, women are still under-represented in science, engineering and technology and only 8 per cent of the engineering workforce and 6 per cent of surgeons are female. On the other hand, only 10 per cent of nurses on the nursing register are male. Social stereotyping might have prevented you from following the course or job you wanted to or may have prevented you from thinking in a wider sense about your options.

Not enough time

Few people have enough time to do all the things they want to do. This is particularly so if you work, have a family and a social life. Studying may be the last thing on your mind and, even if motivated and committed to study, it can be difficult to see how to fit it in with everything else you do. The solution is to use your time as effectively and efficiently as possible, be thoroughly prepared for the degree course, update your study skills, get help from family and friends and remember that studying is not going to last for ever. Most full-time degree courses take three years and it is surprising how quickly this time goes. Many degree courses can be studied part time so do explore this option if you feel it is best for you.

> Don't doubt yourself. You can manage home/work/children so why doubt that you can study/manage your time.
> (Foundation degree in rehabilitation student)

Not enough money

It was much simpler in the past when higher education students received student grants, but the introduction of student loans in 1998 has since caused a lot of financial anxiety about studying in higher education. Choosing to do a degree may involve financial sacrifices, but these will differ depending on your circumstances. A range of financial support related to particular circumstances has been introduced to alleviate some of the anxiety students feel. As part of your planning it is essential to investigate what financial support is available for you. The types of support vary from year to year and are outlined in Chapter 6. Make friends with the student finance team in the university you are interested in and get as much help and advice as you can before you start and also while you are studying. If you are on benefits discuss the implications of returning to study with a benefits adviser to ensure you are aware of the impact on your benefit entitlement. Finally, talk to students who are already studying in higher education and find out how they cope financially.

> It is essential to try and work out how much money you will have coming in and the monies going out. Try to allow yourself the occasional treat – you are going to need it!
>
> (English literature degree graduate)

Not sure what to do

If you did not have advice about job and career options at school you may have found it difficult to make any decisions or focus on your future. There are a variety of organizations offering help and advice for adults who want to change direction, but are unsure what to do. Try to find help by looking in your local telephone book, under 'careers' or 'information services' or call Learndirect (see page 144 for contact details). You should also contact your local university or college as they will probably have careers and advice staff who will be happy to discuss career options with you. There are a number of organizations listed at the end of this book in the section called 'How to get further advice' (page 144).

Too old to do a degree

Quite simply you are never too old to undertake a degree or any level of study. There are more mature students in higher education than ever before and 30 per cent of full-time entrants to higher education and 63 per cent of part-time students are over 30 years old. Employers value mature students who often have more flexible attitudes to work, good interpersonal skills and show commitment and stability.

Don't be put off by being mature – it's just a number. Do not constantly refer to your age. You know how old you are, don't go on about it as then it can define you. The adage of 'as young as you feel' can ring true here.

(Theatre, film and television degree student)

Lack of confidence in your ability

If you have not studied for some time you may feel unsure about your ability to study and worried about coping academically. This may be made worse if your previous experience of education was negative or if you feel that you did not achieve much in your earlier studies. The secret is in the preparation and once again it is important to get help and advice about what to expect, how you need to prepare for your degree and what will be expected of you. Be realistic about what you can achieve in your studies and about your future plans, because if you set your sights too high you may feel disappointed or that you have failed. Try to plan ahead so you have time to update skills or acquire new ones to help you succeed in your degree studies. Don't under-estimate the skills you already have and the competences you have shown in your work or at home. Chapters 3, 4 and 8 cover preparation for higher education in more detail.

New experiences

You may feel daunted by some aspects of returning to study such as working in groups and meeting new people. However, it is likely you have been in a situation where you met new people before, for example, starting a new job. Try to think about how you coped in that situation, what helped you feel at ease and at which point you felt a sense of belonging. Give yourself time to settle into your studies and remember that any change feels strange at first and all students are likely to feel the same.

Need extra support

You may have particular support needs, such as a disability, which you feel would not be addressed if you return to study. Previous experience may have reinforced this feeling and this might cause some anxiety about whether a new experience would be the same. There is a statutory right of access to further and higher education and this, together with a greater awareness of support for people with particular support requirements, should result in a more positive experience this time around. There is a range of financial support for people with disabilities (see Chapter 6) and a range of student support services available (see Chapter 10).

Anxious about change

Some people actively seek change in their lives while others are happy to continue with what they know and feel secure in doing so. Returning to study will involve change and you may find that prospect daunting. If you prepare thoroughly and have realistic expectations you will avoid surprises and be ready for your studies. Remind yourself why you are thinking of returning to study and what you hope to gain from the experience. Reassure yourself that not all aspects of your life will be changing and while you study some things in your life will remain the same.

Study skills need updating

Improve your confidence in your ability by updating your study skills. This includes learning how to write essays and reports, how to prepare for exams and how to use a library and research information. If you have not studied for some time you will probably need to attend a refresher study skills course or a suitable preparatory course. Chapter 4 provides advice on what sort of study skills you will need and Chapter 8 outlines suitable courses to prepare you for higher education.

Computer skills need updating

You may feel less than confident about your ability to use information technology (IT). However, you will not be the only mature student who feels anxious about these skills. Try to enrol on an IT course and check out what is available locally. There is usually a wide range offered in adult education centres and further education colleges and

Learndirect (see page 144) should be able to help you find a suitable course. Make sure this is at the right level for you as there is no point embarking on an advanced IT course if your skills are at a beginner's level. The best course will be one designed for adults who want to return to study and taught by a tutor who appreciates and understands how you feel. Take small steps at first and try not to commit to a long course which you will find daunting or may not have the time to do. Do not try to learn everything at once, take it slowly and recognize your achievements as you progress through the course.

Transport

Sometimes there are geographical barriers to studying and it can be difficult to see how this problem can be overcome. Some students move closer to the place in which they will be studying, but mature students cannot always do this because of family, work and school commitments. If the course you want to do is offered in a local university, but it is difficult and expensive for you to get there, speak to university staff to find out if there are lift-sharing schemes or bursaries to help with travel costs. Always take into account time spent travelling when you are trying to decide whether to study full time or part time. If you cannot overcome transport problems consider the option of undertaking a degree course by distance learning. Distance learning is a flexible way of studying at home and is described in more detail in Chapter 5.

Family and friends

The decisions you make about your future are likely to affect people you are close to, such as your family and friends. Spend time thinking about how they will react to what you want to do and how it will impact on them. You may encounter resistance from family and friends if they have not been included in your decisions or if they feel unsure about the implications. If you involve them they may be able to offer help and encouragement.

- Ask your family how they feel about you studying and doing something different. They will need to support you and will need to understand why you are doing it.

- Tell your friends that you will not have as much spare time as you used to. They may be able to help you with your studies by proof-reading your work.
- Let your work colleagues know what you are doing and why you are doing it.

Returning to study will be a significant change in your life and is going to affect other people as well as yourself. It helps to think about this in advance because if you are aware of the implications of returning to study you are more able to deal with them. If any implications appear to be negative apply some creative thinking to the problem to find a solution.

> My husband helped me make the decision to do a degree. He had studied for an Open University degree, and trained as a nurse in his 40s, so knew all about the pitfalls of studying as a mature student. He offered unequivocal support.
>
> (Theatre, film and television degree graduate)

Essay and exam anxiety

These are two common causes of concern for students, but you may not be able to avoid doing them as part of your degree course. However, some courses do not use exams to assess students. Chapter 4 looks at ways in which to cope with anxieties about essays and exams.

Managing change

Change can sometimes cause stress and anxiety. Some changes are forced upon us such as redundancy, bereavement or health problems. In these cases we may feel we have lost control over our lives and it becomes difficult to cope, especially if the change happens quickly and without much warning.

Often we initiate change through decisions we make. Even so, in a situation where we have made a decision to do something different, we may still feel anxious about the future and how the decision will affect us. Change often means uncertainty and a degree of risk taking.

It is important to ask yourself some questions about any change you are considering:

- Why should I make this change and what do I want out of it?
- If I do not make this change what will happen?
- What will help me make this change?

There are steps you can take to make your return to study untroubled and enjoyable.

Be prepared

Find out what you need to do to bring about the change you want. Think about what you personally will need to do and what other people will need to do.

Plan carefully

Don't rush into a decision. Try to start planning at least one year ahead. If you want to do a degree you will probably have to start your course in Autumn; the traditional start to the academic year. If you have to obtain further qualifications to get on the degree course you want to do then planning ahead will give you time to find an appropriate course and enrol on it. You can also get as much help and advice as you need over the year before you start your degree. Make an action plan stating what you need to do and when, keep reviewing your plan as you go along and be prepared to revise and change it if necessary. Do not expect to be able to plan for every eventuality.

Be realistic

Don't expect too much of yourself and try not to underestimate what you are doing. Bear in mind that if you choose to study you may have to choose not to do something else you currently do. Don't expect life to continue as it is now. Be realistic about the expectations of you as a higher education student; it will involve hard work, challenges, essays, exams and making some sacrifices for the duration of your course.

Be prepared to take a risk

You may find it difficult to make the decision to return to study, but in the future may regret not making it. Sometimes you have to go with your instincts and trust yourself to make the right decision. If you spend time planning and get help and advice along the way the decision you make becomes less of a risk. If you get advice and choose to ignore it, take responsibility for your decisions, do your best and see what happens.

Welcome the positive aspects of change

Do not be daunted by change. Remember that you made the decision to return to study and you have made this decision based on the fact that you can see benefits in doing so. Your studies will hopefully give you a challenge in a positive way, introduce you to a group of new friends, build your confidence and give you some control as well as enabling you to gain a qualification.

Get help, advice and support

The importance of this cannot be overemphasized. Don't tackle this on your own; find out as much as you can and discuss options with as many people as you can.

> The support I received from advice staff in Future Prospects in York was just right. They eased me into every stage and assisted me with childcare issues and my own personal barriers, supporting and encouraging me, constantly building up my confidence and self worth.
>
> (Drama degree student)

You will need to estimate how your life is likely to change:

- You may have less money, less time and need to do things in a different way to the way you did them before.
- You may need to change your hours at work to accommodate your plans, or even stop working altogether, and this will affect you financially.

- You will need to put aside time to devote to your studies and will need to think about the amount of spare time you have now.

Spend time thinking about these issues as this will help your planning and preparation and ensure that you are realistic about your studies and how studying will affect your life. Remember, you will not be studying forever and any sacrifices you make now are for the short term in order hopefully to have a long-term gain.

Dealing with anxiety

> I was worried about studying at degree level, having the communication skills to be able to talk to people and working with students a lot younger than myself, but I was looking forward to meeting people who had similar interests.
>
> (English literature degree graduate)

It is normal to feel some anxiety about your plans and this is an indication that you are thinking carefully about what you intend to do. It is better to deal with any anxieties before you start rather than find yourself surprised by anxieties once you begin your course.

Go through the list below and make a note of any of the anxieties you identify with in relation to returning to study.

Speaking out in a group
Meeting new people
Being confident in your ability
Meeting deadlines
Being organized
Coping with the challenges of a job and study
Managing and planning time
Travelling to university for lectures and seminars
Finance
Giving up a job
Writing an essay
Reading academic textbooks
Writing reports
Using a library and researching information
Coping with lectures
Listening and reading skills

Spelling and grammar
Using a computer
Understanding the subject
Understanding academic jargon
Understanding complex concepts
Critical and creative thinking
Making decisions
Making time for the family
Organizing childcare
Motivation
Self-discipline

Try to relate the anxieties you have identified to situations you have already experienced. For example, if the thought of meeting deadlines makes you anxious, think about any occasions at work when you have had to meet a deadline. How did you cope with this and did you manage to meet the deadline? What did you learn from your experience?

Now prioritize your anxieties and select your top ten – the ones you are most anxious about. Spend some time writing down possible solutions to these.

Remember:

- Most people will feel anxious.
- It will take time to settle in.
- You can ask for support from friends, family and other students.
- Focus on your strengths and use these to help tackle your anxieties.
- Talk to other people – share your problems.
- Make time to relax.

Some anxiety and stress helps to keep you focused, but too much stress can affect your mental and physical health. Recognize the signs of stress, find ways of reducing stress and this will help you while you study.

What next?

You have now identified some of the barriers that might prevent you from studying, but can also see a way of overcoming them. It might take time to do so and you will need to carry on with your planning and preparation. You have also reflected on how to manage change and in particular your return to study and how to deal with any anxieties you have.

The next chapter covers preparation for study. It explains how to identify your current skills and outlines some of the skills you will need while you study.

3

PREPARATION FOR STUDY

This chapter will help you:

- recognize your current skills;
- identify what you have learnt from your experiences so far and relate this to studying;
- identify the skills needed for higher education study;
- be aware of the importance of critical and creative thinking.

Future plans and expectations need to be managed from the outset.

(Sociology and library and information studies degree graduate)

Introduction

Before you begin your course you need to make sure you are thoroughly prepared and ready for study at degree level. This chapter will help you do this by encouraging you to look at your current skills and relate these to skills you need while you study your degree. You will also find out how you can become a critical and creative thinker.

Assessing personal skills

Your life and work experience so far has equipped you with a variety of skills used in a number of situations. You may not be aware of these skills but probably use them frequently. Identifying and reflecting on these is a valuable exercise because you begin to recognize your strengths and how you can apply these to your studies. This will help you gain confidence in your ability to study and to deal with change. In addition, when you start to look for work after the degree course has finished you will need to show employers that you are aware of your strengths and how you can apply them in the workplace.

Current skills

Imagine you have worked for 15 years in a busy solicitors' office, typing correspondence, answering the phone when clients ring, organizing filing, keeping appointment diaries for the solicitors and ensuring the smooth running of the office. You now want to return to study, but it is 20 years since you last studied and that was when you were at school.

The following skills will be required to help you succeed in your studies:

- an ability to meet deadlines for submitting course work to tutors;
- an ability to organize lecture notes and handouts to ensure you can find them when you need them;
- An ability to work in a group with fellow students from a range of backgrounds.

Think about the skills needed to do the job in the office, some of which relate to the study skills listed above. Have a look at the suggestions given below.

- There are strict time scales in a solicitors' office for sending and dealing with correspondence. This requires an ability to meet deadlines.
- The filing system in the solicitors' office needs to be carefully organized to allow referral to files if required. This is particularly so in the case of legal documents. This requires an ability to organize a variety of information in a logical way.
- Dealing with client calls and enquiries involves speaking to a range

of people from varying backgrounds. This experience helps to develop communication skills and diplomacy when it comes to dealing with difficult clients and relates to an ability to work in a group with a variety of people.

Now spend some time thinking about instances from your own life, which illustrate this and which are relevant to meeting deadlines, organizing information and working with people. Look at skills you use in the workplace and at home with your family and think about how they transfer to other situations.

You might have chosen any of the following:

- Getting children to school, paying bills and completing work on time are all examples of meeting deadlines.
- Keeping household records, organizing a family holiday, filing at work and saving documents on your home computer are all examples of organizing information.
- Liaising with colleagues in your workplace, getting on with your neighbours, dealing with a family crisis and giving advice to your children are all examples of working with people.

Many mature students have time management skills, budget management skills and interpersonal skills developed from family, life and work experience. These are often transferable to another situation even if at first they do not appear to be. As you progress through your studies recognize existing skills you can use, perhaps in a different way, and acknowledge new skills as you acquire them.

Make the most of what you already have, but remember why you want to do a degree course. You will be introduced to new ideas and concepts related to the subject you choose to study and will be encouraged to think in a different way while you study.

Personal qualities

What sort of person are you? Pick ten words from the list below which most describe your personal qualities. Be honest with yourself.

sympathetic	practical	assertive
determined	open minded	independent
patient	even tempered	competitive
careful	considerate	persuasive
anxious	adventurous	demonstrative
calm	cautious	cheerful
reliable	sensitive	resilient

Relate different qualities to different jobs. You need to be competitive to be an actor, patient to be a teacher and sensitive to be a good nurse. Be aware of your personal qualities when you are thinking about the job and course you want to do. Get some advice as there are a range of career assessment tools which look at your abilities, interests and personality and then help you identify suitable jobs.

Turn negatives into positives

Few of us are good at self-reflection and recognizing our strengths. It can be difficult sometimes to see any good in some previous experiences, but almost every experience can be viewed positively with a little bit of thought (and imagination).

- Maybe you have had a lot of different jobs and have not stayed in them for long periods of time. This might have been a necessity brought about by having a family or by moving house. By doing a variety of jobs you will be used to new situations and to meeting new people and will be adaptable and open to change.
- Perhaps you have had a lot of low paid jobs. This doesn't mean they were jobs of little worth as many worthwhile jobs are financially undervalued. Concentrate on what you did, not on what you earned. Consider yourself motivated by hard work and not daunted by low pay.
- Maybe you have had little paid work experience, but some voluntary experience. You are not motivated entirely by money and are prepared to do something worthwhile for no financial reward. Your voluntary work will have equipped you with a range of skills.
- Perhaps you have spent the last few years at home looking after your family. Don't undervalue this role just because you feel that others may do. Emphasize the careful decision you made to stay at home, why you value that decision and why it was right for you. Compare

running a house and family to that of a small organization; you did the administration, organization and household budget management and provided motivation and support for your family.

What skills will you need when you study a degree?

There are a number of skills essential to successful study and you may already have some of these.

Organizational skills

Before you begin your degree organize a space at home for your studies, preferably to be used only by you. You will need to make space for any academic text books recommended by your tutors. Find a logical way to organize notes, handouts and photocopies using folders and box files, and label everything. Your filing system should not be too complicated and should be easily understood, especially by you. Buy a dictionary, a thesaurus and a grammar and punctuation guide.

Let your family know that when you study you would prefer not to be interrupted and if this is going to be difficult arrange to go to a friend's house to study.

It is useful to have your own computer as you will be expected to word-process your work and computers make it easier for you to edit your work. It will be even more useful if you know how to use a computer! Make sure your computing skills are up to date by doing a refresher course before you start your degree.

Communication skills

Approximately 75 per cent of our day is spent communicating by speaking, listening, reading and writing, with family, friends and colleagues. Think about situations in which you have communicated with people at work and the skills you used to make that communication effective.

Many jobs involve dealing with a variety of people some of whom may be demanding, insistent or unpleasant. Have you had to deal with anyone in a situation like this and how did you do it? You probably used a variety of communication skills such as diplomacy, tact, politeness, negotiation, persuasion and a number of approaches to diffuse difficult situations. In any type of communication you are going to use different skills and approaches depending on the situation and may need to make quick decisions on how you are going to deal with it. Spend time from now on reflecting on how you communicate and which approaches you take. If you feel there was a breakdown in communication think about why this might have happened and what steps you would take next time to prevent a repeat of this. When you study you are likely to be involved in group work communicating with a variety of different people.

Listening skills

About half of our communication time is spent listening and some jobs, such as those in healthcare, charity or voluntary organizations and working with children or with vulnerable adults, need enhanced listening skills. Organizing your family on a daily basis involves effective listening, otherwise you will never know where everyone is. Think about situations in your own life in which you have had to pay particular care to listening; such as receiving instructions from your manager or receiving information over the phone. Did you listen and understand what was being said? If not, think about what might have helped you improve your listening skills.

When you study you will spend a lot of time listening in lectures so you may need to develop your listening skills. Effective listening involves paying attention, ignoring distractions, understanding the information and message and remembering the information. Hargie *et al.* (1987: 163) state that 'listening is not something that happens physically in the ears, but rather happens mentally between the ears'.

There are many reasons why listening may not be effective. These include background noise, the environment, a distracting speaker, feeling daunted by the situation, having a hearing impairment, being confused or bored or showing personal bias towards the speaker or the topic.

Improve your listening skills by facing the person who is speaking, looking at them and noting their body language. Non-verbal communication such as eye contact, facial expression, nodding and posture is important and can provide many clues to the speaker's message. Put aside any bias you may feel about the speaker, the way they look or talk, and do not let your own opinions affect your judgement. Be a critical and creative thinker by being open to new ideas and opinions.

Teamwork

None of us can function completely on our own and most of us have support networks consisting of friends, family and work colleagues. At work we are likely to be part of a team with particular aims and each person has a role in helping the team achieve these aims.

When you do a degree you will be part of a new team consisting of fellow students who need your support and who will support you. Some of the assessed work on your course might be group work, such as a group presentation, where each member of the group has an equal part to play and your assessment depends on the group working together effectively. You may also find that you work with different groups as you study new topics within your degree course.

Think about a previous situation when you worked in and accomplished something as a team and consider why it worked well. Have you been in any situation in which a team did not work well and, if so, why do you think it did not work?

You will be an effective team member if:

- you are prepared to listen to other people's points of view;
- you like to encourage and support other people;
- you are prepared to make a contribution;
- you do not react badly to constructive criticism;
- you are ready to admit your mistakes to others and will learn from them.

I soon found that I mixed well with the diverse range of people present in college, probably due to the fact I have always worked with people of all ages and from all walks of life.

(Design and technology degree student)

Presentation skills

You may need to do group or solo presentations as part of your degree. Although many people find this daunting bear in mind that the more presentations you do the more confident you will feel about doing them. To ensure a successful presentation always make sure you know who your audience are and that you have identified what you hope to achieve. Be thoroughly prepared, know your topic and practise your presentation in advance. Keep things simple and try to speak slowly

without reading from detailed notes. It can help you to feel more re-
laxed if you use Powerpoint software or overhead projector slides as
your audience will look at them and not at you.

Problem solving

Problem solving is a daily feature of life with problems ranging from
small and insignificant to large scale and very worrying. It is normal to
have problems, but we do not always find the right way to deal with
them or solve them. Think about any problems you encountered
during the last week. How did you identify them? What solutions did
you find? Did the solutions solve the problems?

Reflect on whether you are a natural problem solver. If people often
tell you their problems and ask for help you are probably not only a
good listener, but also a good problem solver.

To be an effective problem solver you need to be calm, open to new
ideas and opinions and ready to take different approaches. You need to
be able to identify the root of the problem you need to solve and then
consider a variety of different approaches to it and evaluate which one
or ones may work best. Think about what you may need to help you
solve the problem and then identify which solution you are going to
adopt. Try it out and reflect on the outcome. If the problem is solved
your approach was the right one (this time). If the problem is still
outstanding you might need to find another solution and look at it
from a different angle. Do not give up, but try something else.

When you study you are likely to encounter problems. Your studies
might result in a lack of time for your family or difficulty with budgeting. Or you may find it difficult to understand a particular concept
or idea or have difficulty meeting an assignment deadline. You might
be given problem-solving exercises to do as an assessed part of your
course.

Time management

Mature students benefit from varied previous experiences and, for
many who work and have families, this includes time management.
The secret of successful time management is to make the most effective
and efficient use of your available time.

Think about whether you are a good manager of time or whether you have problems keeping to time, meeting deadlines, remembering commitments and generally spend your life in a rush trying to get from place to place. Note down how you use time and what problems, if any, you have in organizing your time. If you feel you have problems with time management try to start improving your skills in this area. You will have less time once you start studying so work at making the most of the time you have.

When planning your time think about what you need to achieve each day and week and identify priorities. Once you have done this think about the amount of time you need to be able to achieve these priorities. Then reflect on how much time you waste and what you are wasting it on and identify what you can rearrange or cut out.

How to improve your time management when you study:

- Update your study skills, computer skills and library skills before your degree course.
- Write all lectures, seminars, tutorials, exam dates in a diary and refer to it!
- Find out from academic staff how much work they expect you to undertake each week.
- Find a time for your independent study which suits you and which you know will be a good time to study. This might be in the morning when you feel refreshed or in the evening after children have gone to bed.
- Do challenging work when you feel alert, not when you feel tired.
- Study in chunks of time and, as a guide, take a 10 minute break every hour you study as this will help your concentration.
- Share study tasks, such as photocopying, taking notes or researching information, with fellow students.
- Plan how long each study task will take and don't underestimate the time you need. As you progress in your studies you will gain a better understanding of how long you need to spend in the library or how long it takes to plan an essay.
- Keep a balance between studying and leisure time and don't neglect either.
- Be prepared for the unexpected to happen. Don't panic if you have to change your study plans; use your problem-solving skills and find solutions.

I realize that I have learnt a great deal more than just reading a book or sketching and drawing a picture, such as researching projects and managing my time better in order to spend time with my family instead of devoting every waking hour to the college. I can now prioritize tasks, in order to meet the deadlines in time, without having left things until the last minute.

(Design and technology degree student)

Task management

Divide study tasks such as essay writing into chunks as this makes the task more manageable and achievable. It helps you set a start and end point and gives you a checklist for action you need to take along the way. This makes you focus on the task and gives goals to aim for. As you reach each goal you gain a sense of achievement and this helps to keep you motivated.

Independent learning

Mature students are often surprised by the amount of time each week devoted to attending lectures. Some degree courses may only have 8 to 10 hours of lectures and seminars each week, although this varies from course to course. However, do not be misled into an expectation of having a lot of spare time.

You may find that your studying is less structured than previous experiences and this can be difficult to cope with at first. Degree study promotes independent learning by which it expects you to do your reading, research and assignments in your own time. This requires motivation, self-discipline, decision making, planning, prioritizing and taking responsibility for your own learning. As you progress through your degree course you will be expected to become more independent in your studies and the work will become more challenging.

To be a successful independent learner you need to be motivated and acquire self-discipline. Keep thinking about what has motivated you to return to study. Plan your independent study by setting goals and start dates for particular tasks so you avoid procrastination. Note your achievements as you reach each goal you have set. It is easy to feel isolated and to lose direction when your study involves independent learning. If you feel this way, talk to your tutors at university or get help from your fellow students.

Memory skills

If you consider yourself to be mature you may subscribe to the idea that memory capacity diminishes with age. However, this view is not necessarily substantiated by research carried out into memory and age. It may be that as we get older we become more familiar with what we are doing each day, such as our job or daily routine, and do not use our memory skills to their full extent.

How to improve your memory:

- Ask yourself questions as you learn.
- Use visual cues to remember your learning.
- Make your notes of lectures, books and journals interesting to read by using colour or pictures.
- Relate your learning to your experience to make sense and place it in context.
- Use devices which help the memory, such as mnemonics. A good example of mnemonics is 'Richard Of York Gave Battle In Vain' where the capital letter of each word refers to the colours of the rainbow in order.
- Use repetition by going over your learning.
- Discuss your work with fellow students and share ideas.
- Keep reviewing your work.

Critical and creative thinking

Studying at degree level in a university will be a different experience to those you had at school or college. During your degree you will be introduced to differing viewpoints from your tutor, your fellow students and from reading academic text books related to your subject. You will be expected to develop understanding of your subject by thinking critically and creatively.

Aim to be a critical thinker by:

- questioning your learning and not taking things at face value;
- learning to challenge ideas, both yours and any others you are introduced to;
- examining evidence and identifying bias or assumptions, including your own;
- being open to different opinions.

Aim to be a creative thinker by:

- being open and inventive in your learning;
- being different in the approaches you take and trying new approaches to see if they work;
- being open to change, either in your own opinions or the way you approach your learning.

There are examples throughout history of theories and concepts, which were thought to be true, but which were eventually challenged and found to be unsound. Often these relate to medicine and science when quite flawed views have been accepted as the truth, only to be challenged later on and disproved. It was only because people were prepared to question and challenge assumptions that new discoveries were made and continue to be made.

Question and challenge

Imagine you have picked up a leaflet about local government spending which emphasizes how much money has been spent on children's playgrounds in your area over the last year. It sounds impressive and large sums of money are mentioned, but consider the following:

- Who wrote the leaflet? Are they biased? Do they have a point to prove? The author may be a member of a local political party who is seeking re-election.
- Large sums of money are mentioned. Does the leaflet provide a comparison with how much money was spent the year before so you have evidence of an increase in spending?
- Why has the leaflet been published? There may be a local election ahead and the leaflet is part of a political campaign.
- Does the leaflet seem that impressive now? Can you rely on the evidence in it or do you feel there are more questions you need to ask?

You may already be using critical and creative skills in your workplace or at home without realizing you are doing so. Think about some recent problems you have had to deal with and resolve. Did you consider new ways of thinking and a new approach and, if so, what was the outcome of your new approach?

There are many books available on critical and creative thinking and some are listed in the section on Recommended Reading at the end of the book.

What next?

This chapter has covered some of the skills needed for successful study and some of the ways in which you can prepare yourself for your degree course. The next chapter will introduce you to some of the study skills essential for degree level study, such as essay writing, taking notes and how to cope with exams.

4

STUDY SKILLS

This chapter will help you:

- understand what is meant by study skills;
- identify some of the study skills essential for degree level study.

Introduction

Study skills help you learn and study effectively. Think about water-colour painting or doing home repairs. It is best not to start either of these without some idea of the techniques used. For example, if you want to take up watercolour painting you will need to find out what paints to buy, what type of brushes are best and how to mix colours. If you don't do this then your painting efforts may not work. Similarly, if you intend to put in a new bathroom and do not find out how plumbing works you might find yourself in trouble.

Study skills involve understanding techniques relating to essay and report writing, taking notes, researching information, revising for exams, listening to lectures, making a presentation, reading course books and organizing your work. Your skills in each area will improve as you progress through your course.

Your study routine involves where, how and when you study and the way you organize your study time. There is no right or wrong way of doing this as long as you recognize what works best for you and make the most effective use of your time. For example, will you do your reading at home, or in the library or in a cafe? You will probably choose a location where you feel comfortable and are free from interruptions and will have certain times during the day when you study best.

Lastly, study skills involve the use of processes to help you understand what you are studying. You should be prepared to think about your studies, take in and analyse new information, reflect on it, relate it to previous experience, understand it and express ideas.

Study skills are important for a number of reasons:

- Your study routine helps you manage your time and become an independent learner.
- This helps you organize your work.
- The techniques help you manage assignments.
- The processes encourage you to think, reflect and understand.
- Your studying becomes more effective and successful.
- You feel more confident in your ability to study and to complete your course.

Researching information

You will be expected to draw on a variety of resources (books, journals, the Internet) to support your studies and increase your knowledge in the subject you are studying. Your tutors will not want to read a list of your own thoughts and ideas, but will be looking for an ability to research information, understand other people's opinions and research and use it to inform your work. If your tutor has provided a reading list related to your degree make sure you refer to it as you will not have time to consult every book in the library which relates to your subject. Take a note of the resources you are using so you can refer to them again if you need to. It can be easy to forget where you found interesting material if you don't make a note of the author, title, date of publication and where you found it.

When you start your course you should be offered a library induction, which usually involves a group tour of the library and a brief explanation about how the resources in the library are organized. Make sure you attend the induction as academic libraries can sometimes be confusing places and it can be difficult to know where to start searching for information.

Always check the library opening times and do not underestimate how much time you may need to do an information search. Make sure you understand what it is you are looking for, why you want it and what you are expected to achieve. If you are looking for information relating to an assignment, such as an essay or report, and you are unsure what the assignment is about, ask your tutor before visiting the library. Do not be afraid to ask library staff for assistance and make an appointment if you feel you need a lot of help.

Use information carefully and make sure it is relevant, up to date and accurate. Learn to evaluate what you read and remember the section on critical thinking in Chapter 3. Do not take everything at face value and when you are reading ask yourself the following questions:

- Who is the author, have they published other work and are they an expert in the subject area?
- Is the publisher reliable and reputable?
- Is the information up to date?
- Is the information biased in any way? If so, how and why?
- Does it cover the subject in depth or is anything missing?
- Does it represent fact or opinion? If it represents opinion, whose opinion?
- Why was it written and for whom?
- Is there a hidden meaning?
- Is it easy to use and well presented?

Referencing and bibliographies

When doing assignments, such as essays or reports, you will be expected to refer to your reading to support the points you make in your work. Your tutors will expect references to authors and experts in the field and evidence that you are building up knowledge of your subject. If you refer to authors and information you have read you will be expected to acknowledge this by using a system known as referencing and producing a bibliography which is essentially a list of the books, journals and Internet sites which have helped inform your work. The most common system of referencing is the Harvard system. Find out which system your university uses and make sure you follow this when you produce work for assessment. It is important to acknowledge other authors' work as this will avoid any accusations of plagiarism or presenting other work as your own. See Creme and Lea (1997) for more detail on the Harvard system and other systems of referencing.

Reading skills

You will probably read some challenging, interesting and thought-provoking books and journals when you study. Unfortunately you will also read some thoroughly uninspiring material and this will challenge you in a different way!

Academic books and journals help increase your subject knowledge, but you might find it difficult to take in all the information and will need to concentrate while you read. The academic style of writing and the language used may differ from books you have read before and the level of recall will need to be higher than you expect when reading for leisure.

You may encounter complex language and concepts and if you find it hard to understand it can be difficult to remain interested. As with any reading you may find an author's style of writing difficult and will probably prefer some authors to others. However, you will be expected to read recommended texts and will not always be able to pick and choose what you read. If you are given a reading list you will be expected to consult the books on it, especially if any of them are written by your tutor! However, you will not have the time to read everything from cover to cover.

Start to improve your reading skills by reading a newspaper article, or part of a book, and when you finish consider the following.

- Did it take long to read?
- Did you find it interesting?
- Can you recall what you have read and summarize it in one or two sentences?
- Did you find it difficult to read? If so, why?
- Was there a lot of jargon and words you didn't understand?
- Did you enjoy the style of writing?
- What did you like or dislike about this style?

Reading techniques

There are a number of reading techniques you can use:

- *Inspection* provides a general idea about a book as you examine the back cover, contents page, index and chapter headings. Inspection helps you decide if the book is relevant to your needs without reading it in great detail.

- *Scanning* helps you focus on key words, headings, sub-headings, diagrams and tables and provides a general idea of the material and of the style of writing.
- *Skimming* involves looking quickly through the actual text itself, perhaps reading introductory paragraphs in chapters and becoming familiar with the book's content.
- *Intensive study reading* involves gaining a full understanding of the text. You need to concentrate to do this and will need to review your reading and test your recall of information.

How to improve your reading skills

The first thing to do is have your eyes tested if you have difficulty seeing the text. Always set a time limit for your reading and make sure you take breaks to help your concentration. If you come across words you don't understand look them up in a dictionary and compile a glossary of words and terms relating to your subject. Use the right reading technique at the right time and vary the speed of your reading according to the resource and your aim. Read slowly if the text is complex or full of detail, for example law and medical books. Your reading will speed up as you develop your subject knowledge.

Taking notes

During your degree you will need to take notes at lectures and from books and journals. Taking notes helps you organize information and ideas, provides you with information to refer to later on, helps you complete assignments such as essays and helps you revise for examinations. The process of taking notes makes you think about what you are learning and keeps you focussed on your learning. Taking notes in a lecture ensures you stay alert and focused, particularly important if you find the lecture topic (or lecturer) boring.

You have probably taken notes at work, for example taking minutes at a meeting or taking notes from a phone call. Think about some recent situations in which you have taken notes. Why did you take notes, what did you use them for and were they useful?

Taking notes in a lecture

Try to go to all lectures. They are informative and clarify the reading materials used for the coursework.

(Theatre, film and television degree graduate)

Your listening skills may be tested in a lecture as some can last for one or two hours and involve the lecturer passing lots of information to students. You may have a handout summarizing the main points of the lecture, but will probably be expected to take notes as well. It is essential to be able to read and understand your notes afterwards otherwise any time spent taking them will be wasted. There are ways in which you can improve the quality of your lecture notes:

- Make sure you can hear the speaker! It also helps if you can see them as well.
- Do advance reading before the lecture if you have been asked to do so as this will help you understand the topic of the lecture.
- Make sure you are familiar with jargon and keywords relevant to the subject.
- Write the date and time of the lecture, the topic and the name of the lecturer on your notes.
- Leave space in your notes so you can add more notes later on if you need to.
- Ask questions if you do not understand what the lecturer is saying.
- Don't write down everything said, but note key points and general ideas, using sub-headings to organize these ideas.
- Pick up pointers from the lecturer. If they state three main points, make a note of all three.
- Be accurate about noting important facts, figures or references to authors.
- Use abbreviations if they help, but make sure you understand them later.
- Read through your notes as soon after the lecture as possible and make amendments if you need to.
- Organize your notes in a logical way so you can refer to them later.

Taking notes from resources such as books, journals, articles and handouts

You will be expected to read a variety of resources while you study and will need to take notes from any which are of particular relevance to your subject. There are ways in which you can improve the quality of your notes from books, journals, articles and handouts:

• Your course should be structured so you start off with easier material first to help you develop your subject knowledge.
• Look at the contents page, index pages and chapter headings of resources to help you decide if they are relevant to your needs.
• Consider why you are reading the material and what you expect to get out of it. Are you trying to complete an assignment and are you clear about the information you are looking for?
• Write down the bibliographic details (author, title, publisher, date of publication) of the material you are reading so you can refer to the resource later.
• Leave space in your notes so you can add more notes later if you need to.
• Note frequently used key words and phrases.
• Use headings and sub-headings for key points to help organize your notes.
• Use your own words to summarize as this will help you recall the information.
• Record all facts and figures accurately.
• If you own the resource underline or highlight key words on the page. This helps you remember them and helps you refer back later on.

Methods of note taking

There are a variety of note-taking methods and you should use whatever method you prefer. Any good study skills book will outline methods of note taking and provide examples. Methods include mind maps, spider diagrams, linear or bullet points, pattern notes using visual images or index cards. There is no right or wrong way as long as your notes are clear and you can understand them.

Essay writing

Many students feel anxious about writing essays particularly if they have not done so for a long period of time. As with any study skill your essay writing will improve with practice and you should get a lot of practice on a degree course.

Essays are frequently used in higher education to test subject knowledge, develop research and analytical skills and improve writing skills. You are likely to have essays varying in length, in most cases will be given a title to work to and will be expected to produce a piece of formal, academic writing relating to that title. This should enable you to remember the subject you are writing about and it should make you think about concepts related to that subject.

Most essays will be handed in to a tutor for assessment and you should receive feedback from the tutor about how well (or otherwise) you have done. This will help your tutor assess your progress on the course.

An essay should have a title, a deadline for submission, a stated word length, an introduction, a discussion or argument, a conclusion, a reference list and a bibliography.

Essay planning

This is an essential stage in putting together your essay and one that is often neglected in the haste to start writing. Planning time is time well spent and if you do not plan properly you might not fully understand the essay title and might not produce a piece of work related to that title.

To begin you should look carefully at the essay title and underline what you think are the key words in it. These words provide an indication of what you are supposed to be writing about and what tone you should adopt in your essay.

> Read the question! Break the title down. Keep referring to the title throughout which helps you keep on track, helps direct your response, makes the essay flow.
>
> (Foundation degree in rehabilitation student)

Some key words are used frequently in essay titles and the list below provides a definition of some of the most common ones.

Account for	Describe how and why something happened
Analyse	Look at in detail
Compare	Identify similarities
Contrast	Identify differences
Describe	Provide an outline of the topic
Discuss	Look at important features of a topic
Evaluate	Appraise or assess something
Examine	Look at a subject in detail
Explain	Outline why something happens or what something means
Illustrate	Clarify giving examples
Justify	Support an argument

Break your essay writing task into manageable chunks, taking into account your deadline, and set yourself a start date, time for researching information, time for reading, writing time and proof-reading. Make sure you can use a library so you are able to get the information you need. Then write down as many of your thoughts as possible about the essay title and link your ideas together to get a structure to your thoughts. This helps you come up with initial ideas on the essay topic and can be kept as a working document you can add to or delete ideas from. You might not use all the notes you make, but at least you have started to think about the topic. This will also help you narrow down a large topic and gain a focus for your essay.

Essay presentation

Your university should produce guidelines on essay presentation. These may differ from department to department and from tutor to tutor, but as long as you have guidelines make sure you use them. Take advice about whether you should word-process your essay or whether the university accepts handwritten essays. Using a computer to produce your essay makes it easier to edit and rewrite.

Essay style

Correct use of punctuation and grammar helps your essay style and improves your writing. Be careful not to use slang or informal language unless you are using this to illustrate a point. It is tempting to use long words to try to impress your tutor, but simple language is more ef-fective. Look at the length of your sentences and make sure they are neither too long nor too short. Short sentences make the essay appear too disjointed and long sentences tend to lose their sense by the time you get to the end of them.

Essay introduction

Think about an example of an introduction (to a person, to a novel, to a speech) and how this provides a starting point. An essay introduction introduces your essay topic to the reader. Some students include a definition in their introduction, particularly if there is a word in the essay title needing an explanation. You may put in a quotation, but make sure it is relevant and adds to your essay, rather than putting it in for the sake of it.

When you wrote down all your thoughts on the essay topic you may have decided not to use some of them, but to focus on a particular aspect of the topic. If this is the case you need to explain in your introduction which aspect you are going to look at in your essay (and then make sure that you do look at it!). For example, if you have been asked to write an essay about the meaning of community (a vast sub-ject) you might introduce this as follows:

This essay will discuss the definition of community identity from a cultural and spiritual perspective and will draw on examples to illustrate the points made.

or

This essay will analyse two communities in the South Wales Val-leys and describe how these communities have been affected by the changing nature of employment.

The main part of the essay

This is the largest part of the essay and should include ideas, argu-ments, opinions, facts, research and evidence. It should follow a logical sequence and be easy to read and understand.

Divide your essay into paragraphs and, as a general rule, make one point or theme per paragraph. Use paragraphs to put together similar ideas and to break up the text of the essay. Do not just list the points you want to make, but discuss them in detail. To help your essay flow use linking words and phrases, such as 'however' and 'in addition to this', to ensure that paragraphs are connected and don't stand in isolation. However, try to avoid overuse of such words and phrases and do not repeat points already made.

Use information gathered from research to back up the points you make in the essay. You might be asked to include examples of your own experience especially if your course relies heavily on work-based learning as is the case with many foundation degrees.

Avoid making generalizations and assumptions in your essay. Try not to say 'I think' and 'I believe' unless what you think and believe is backed up by evidence you have found. Do not make sweeping statements which have no basis in fact as your tutor will ask for the evidence to support what you have said. The following are examples of generalizations:

'Most women want to stay at home and would prefer not to go out to work.'

'Many young people think studying is a waste of time.'

'Hardly any money is spent on care services for the elderly.'

All of these statements need facts and figures to back them up. For instance, in the first example, how was this conclusion reached, who did the research and how many women did they ask? How many women as a percentage of all women have stated they want to stay at home?

Essay conclusion

The conclusion sums up all the ideas and evidence used in the essay and should relate to the essay title. No new points should be introduced at this stage. It is important for the conclusion to signal an end to the essay and your reader should have a sense of having come to the end. There may be no definite answer to any question raised in the essay title or any definite case for either side of an argument. Your conclusion might decide that further debate is needed on the topic before a case can be made.

Editing and rewriting

Always make time to do this before your essay deadline. It is vital that you proof-read your essay, not just for any spelling mistakes, but to identify any areas you feel need improvement. Don't be afraid to re-write parts of your essay if you feel you need to, but on the other hand do not spend so long doing this that you miss your deadline. Do a spell check, check punctuation and make sure the essay flows and you have introduced your issues and themes in a logical way (ask someone to read it). Always make sure you have kept within the word length as, although there is often some leeway, you will not get extra marks for writing 3,000 words when you have been asked for 2,000.

Case study

Carl had applied to do a degree course and was supporting his application with evidence of relevant work experience and by doing an essay related to the subject he was hoping to study. He attended as many short study skills and essay writing workshops as possible, some of them at the university he was applying to. By doing this he not only improved his study skills, but also felt integrated into the university community at an earlier stage. He successfully gained a place on his chosen degree course.

Revision skills

> Prepare and try not to panic. If there are sessions on exam tech-niques available take advantage of them even if it is just to confirm that you are working along the right lines.
>
> (English literature degree graduate)

Many mature students say that exams are a source of anxiety. Not everyone is good at exams and they can induce panic among students of any age. Mature students may have less than fond memories of exams at school and may not have done one for many years so revision skills will seem an alien concept to them.

Plan a revision timetable starting well in advance of the exams, and make sure you keep to it. Keep your notes and handouts accessible and try reducing your notes to prompt words or phrases. Revise in short spells so you maintain your concentration. Don't think you can revise everything you have studied so far and try going through some old exam papers and doing a test run. Share your revision with your fellow students and test each other. Finally, make sure you relax, eat and sleep well and don't cut out all leisure time.

Exam skills

Make sure you do the following to ensure success in your exams:

- Get the date and time of the exam right and be punctual.
- Try not to revise all night before the exam.
- Read and re-read the exam paper and check both sides of the exam paper.
- Make sure you follow instructions. Don't answer all questions when you have only been asked to answer four out of ten.
- Cross out questions you have decided not to answer.
- Divide your time up into reading, planning, writing and proof-reading, with some spare time at the end.
- Answer your best question first and get off to a positive start.
- Don't write too much on one question and not enough on another. Try to divide your time equally.
- If you are running out of time and have an unanswered question, or have not finished your answer, do an outline plan of the question, giving main facts, points or formulas, to show what ideas you would have included.
- Write neatly and legibly.

Assessment

Throughout your degree you will be asked to provide evidence of your learning, by doing essays, reports, learning journals, presentations and exams, so your tutor can assess how your studies are progressing. The results of these assessments will form the basis for your final degree result. Try not to take the assessment too personally; your tutor is there to help you and their comments can help you improve your work. Use your feedback as pointers on how you can improve your work in the future and act on suggestions given by your tutors.

If you are not happy with your assessment, or just don't understand some of the points, do go and talk to your tutors about it. They will always be pleased to help you improve your standard of work – it reflects on them after all.

(English literature degree graduate)

What next?

This chapter has outlined some of the study skills required to succeed in higher education. Try to improve these skills before you start your degree.

The next chapter will describe what higher education is and outline the types of course available. It will explain what is expected from higher education students and detail some of the learning and teaching methods used in higher education.

5

WHY HIGHER EDUCATION?

This chapter will help you:

- understand what higher education is;
- understand the difference between the types of course available at higher education level;
- be realistic about what to expect from a higher education course;
- identify the learning and teaching methods used in higher education.

Regrets? Not at all, wish I'd done it 25 years ago.

(History degree graduate)

Introduction

Higher education provides higher level qualifications for people over the age of 18. It includes degree courses, foundation degrees and higher national diplomas. There are also many other courses offered, such as short professional courses and postgraduate courses which students take after completing a degree. Students who are undertaking degree courses are called undergraduates.

Many degree courses lead to specific jobs, such as medicine, law, nursing and physiotherapy, while other degree courses provide a specialism in a subject and a number of options once graduating. For example, English graduates may go into teaching, journalism, librarianship or publishing and history graduates may go into heritage work, archive work or teaching.

Deciding to do a degree course can be a daunting decision for many mature students who have little idea what to expect and whose life while they study is likely to be quite different from their life before. It helps to get all the advice you can before you start as you will then have a realistic idea of what to expect and what is expected of you.

Types of higher education institutions

Higher education institutions include universities, colleges of higher education, colleges of further education and colleges which specialize in art or performance. These institutions vary in size, environment, type of student and, of course, location and it is important to visit a higher education institution prior to applying to ensure you are likely to be happy there.

Universities

Some universities were established hundreds of years ago, for example Oxford was established in the eleventh century and the University of Wales Lampeter was founded in 1822. More recently the University of York was established in 1963. A number of 'new' universities were created following the Further and Higher Education Act 1992. This enabled polytechnics, which primarily offered vocational courses, to acquire university status.

Many are noted for their reputation in a particular subject area, such as science, technology and engineering, sports degrees or business and management. Most higher education institutions have a subject area or a range of subject areas for which they are particularly well regarded.

Colleges of higher education

Colleges of higher education also offer degree courses. These colleges tend to be smaller than most universities and began with a focus on a particular subject area, but now offer a wide range of degree subjects. There are approximately fifty colleges of higher education in the UK.

Specialist higher education institutions

These specialize in a particular subject area such as the Northern School of Contemporary Dance, Falmouth College of Arts or the Central School of Speech and Drama. There are also agricultural colleges, medical schools and law colleges.

Colleges of further education

Some degree courses are offered in further education colleges. These provide a wide range of mainly vocational courses and a number of courses which enable students to prepare for the workplace and for higher education. Their courses are usually available for people aged 16 and over. (See Chapter 8 on preparatory courses for higher education).

There are approximately five hundred institutions in the UK offering over fifty thousand higher education courses. The choice of subjects is therefore vast and there really is something for everyone: from American studies to zoology, surf science to philosophy and English literature to golf course management.

Expansion of higher education

More students are now in higher education than ever before and there has been an increase in the number of full- and part-time students since the 1960s. The number of students participating in higher education increased quite dramatically in the 1980s and 1990s and students over 21 years of age are now well represented, particularly in part-time study.

There are a number of reasons why the number of people engaged in higher education has increased:

- Government policy has encouraged institutions to ensure that more people benefit from the advantages of higher education, in particular people who might not otherwise consider higher education. In some ways higher education is more accessible for students of all ages than it has been in the past, although students from less affluent backgrounds are less likely to go to university.

- Higher education institutions are increasingly encouraged to look for a range of skills and qualities when they receive applications from mature students. This means taking into account work and life experiences as well as any formal qualifications.
- The concept of a job for life is disappearing with an acceptance that people may need to retrain at various stages in their working life. This means that many adults need to learn new skills in order to remain in employment. Increasing use of information technology has changed many jobs and necessitated the acquisition of new skills.
- There is greater acceptance of learning during all stages of life and an importance attached to learning for leisure and well-being.

What are the benefits of doing a degree?

The long term aim was to improve employment prospects.
(Sociology and library and information studies degree graduate)

- Some jobs, for example, teacher, doctor, lawyer, physiotherapist, librarian, engineer, architect and nurse, require higher level qualifications and it is impossible to enter those professions without this qualification.
- Some jobs, which previously did not need a degree qualification, such as nursing and occupational therapy, now ask for applicants to have a degree.
- All degree courses, whether specific to a particular profession or not, provide students with skills required by employers. These skills include problem solving, teamworking, analytical and creative thinking and using initiative. Employers will be interested in your particular degree subject, but may be more interested in the fact that you have undergone study at degree level and have acquired the skills listed above.
- Most degree courses have a vocational element, in that they prepare you for work through the acquisition of specific skills and the inclusion of a work placement as part of the degree course.
- Research has shown that people with degrees earn more over their working life than people without degrees. Be realistic about this though and do some of your own research into your job prospects.

- Higher education allows you to explore a subject of interest in more depth than you will probably have done in the past. It opens up subjects and study in a way quite different from experiences at school or training at work.
- Higher education increases your confidence in your ability for academic study and helps you feel more confident about getting a fulfilling job once you have graduated.
- Lastly, higher education provides a personal challenge for the student.

Types of degree courses

Most full-time degree courses take three years to complete, although some take four years if they include a work placement or year abroad. These are often called 'sandwich' courses and, if they involve a year of work experience, can help to improve job prospects after graduation. The work experience may be salaried, should be supervised and will provide valuable practical experience and professional development.

Some, but not all, degrees are honours degrees. An honours degree requires 360 credits (there is more about credits later on in this chapter; see page 64). Some universities do not put all their students forward for honours degrees, but may do if progress is good. In some Scottish universities an honours degree may take four years, but students can graduate with a general degree after three years.

Foundation degrees are a relatively new type of degree, usually take two years to complete and are equivalent to the first two years of a degree course. After two years students can use the foundation degree as a qualification in its own right or may have the option to progress to the third year of a related degree course. Foundation degrees are often vocational which means they relate to a particular area of work such as teaching or health and social care. There is a strong emphasis on work-based learning, which allows the student to apply their learning to the workplace. Therefore students gain academic knowledge and theory as well as the skills needed to succeed at work. Foundation degrees also provide an opportunity for people already in work to gain skills which will help them progress in their workplace, for example teaching assistants can do a foundation degree to enable them to qualify as teachers.

Higher national diplomas (HNDs) are generally two years of full-time study and are vocational such as art and design, business studies, engineering or computing. They are well regarded as a qualification in their own right or as a route to a degree course and often include valuable work experience. It may be possible to enter the second year of a degree course if you have successfully completed an HND.

Combinations of study

Specialist degree or single honours degrees allow you to study one subject and specialize in that particular subject while at university.

Joint or combined honours degrees allow you to combine two subjects over the duration of your degree so, for example, you could study American studies and journalism or psychology and criminology. This option enables you to study two subjects of particular interest and is useful if you are unable to make up your mind about which subject to study. You should spend equal amounts of time on each subject. Be careful with your choice if you have a particular career in mind as you may need to do a specialist degree for some careers.

Interdisciplinary or multidisciplinary degrees allow you to study more than two subjects, for example European studies. You design your degree programme with the help of academic staff and might then have the option to move to a single or joint degree after your first year of study.

Major/minor degrees mean you will study two subjects but spend more time on one subject than the other, for example you might study business studies with a minor in law.

Length of course

Not all degree courses take three years and you may need to do further study for some professions. Some courses, such as medicine, veterinary medicine and architecture take longer to complete and require years of further study after the initial degree. For example, if you are interested in clinical or educational psychology you will need to undertake further postgraduate training. Students who wish to become primary or secondary school teachers may have a further year of study after their degree finishes. Always do research into the career you are interested in so you have a realistic idea of how long it will take to qualify.

Course structure

It is possible to study many degree courses either full- or part-time and there is now more flexibility to study part-time. However, not all courses are available to study part-time and it is important to investigate the options relating to the course you want to do.

If you study full-time most degrees will take three years to complete or two years in the case of a foundation degree. Some courses, such as teaching or occupational therapy, may include full-time work placements. You may find that you are unable to undertake these courses on a part-time basis.

Part-time study, of course, takes longer than three years. You may take from five to eight years to complete your degree part-time depending on how flexible your chosen university is. It is essential to speak to academic staff to find out how flexible they will be as you may find some tutors who are prepared to structure the course around your needs. Compare the implications of full-time and part-time study before you make a decision about which is best for you and take into account other commitments in your life. You might have the option to switch from full to part-time or vice versa later on in your course.

Contact time in university

It is difficult to give a precise indication of how much contact time you will spend in university, in lectures, seminars and tutorials, as this varies depending on the university and the course. Before applying for full- or part-time study find out how much time you will be expected to be in for lectures and seminars and take into account time spent reading and completing assignments.

Distance learning

Distance learning is a flexible way of study for people who cannot attend university on a regular basis or who are interested in undertaking their study at home. You may be given a minimum and maximum time in which you can finish the course and can then study at your own pace within these guidelines. Most of the study is done independently and it is therefore possible to fit this into a busy home and working life. Your learning will be supported by residential study schools and by IT support and tutor support either on the telephone or in person. Primarily though, the learning will be independent and it is important to take this into account as you will need to be motivated and disciplined in establishing a study routine. You may also feel isolated as you will not spend much time with fellow students.

The Open University provides distance learning courses at degree level and has done since 1971. It is well respected, has good quality learning materials and good support systems for its students, 80 per cent of whom work. There is no time limit on completion of the degree course although most of their students take at least six years to complete.

More universities are developing distance learning courses because of the increasing need for more flexible types of study. It is likely that distance learning will become even more popular as students realize the financial implications of studying in higher education.

How degree courses are organized

Academic year

Generally, most degree courses will run over an academic year, which starts in September/October and finishes in June/July with breaks at Christmas and Easter. However, some courses, such as foundation degrees, start at different times of the year and it is important to get information about the start date of your chosen course. During the academic year you will probably have reading weeks, during which you undertake some background reading relating to your course or revise for forthcoming examinations. A full-time degree is divided into level 1 (the first year), level 2 (the second year) and level 3 (the third year).

Semesters and terms

The academic year will be divided into semesters or terms. The number of these varies from university to university. During each semester or term you will study modules relating to your subject area.

Modules

Modules are a series of short courses, relating to your particular subject area, which build up your knowledge in the subject you are studying. For example, an English degree may include modules about children's literature, American literature or Shakespeare, and a history degree may include modules about the second world war, medieval society or Victorian England. You will study different modules in different semesters or terms.

Most students will begin by studying the same compulsory core modules, which set the scene for the subject. There may be some core modules in each year of the degree and you will be required to take these before you progress to other modules. It is then possible to follow particular areas of interest within your subject area by choosing optional modules and sometimes there is the opportunity to take a module from another subject area.

You will be assessed on your learning on each module in a variety of ways, including writing essays or reports or giving presentations on the subject topic of the module. Each module, in each academic year of study, gives you a number of credits if you pass your assessments. The credits are then added up and your marks for your assessments and the module credits achieved form the basis of your final result.

Credits

Credits are awarded for successful completion of modules and of the assignments related to those modules. If you study full time you need to obtain 120 credits in your first year of study (a Certificate in Higher Education), 120 credits in your second year (a Diploma of Higher Education) and 120 credits in your third year (a degree). This is a nationally agreed system in the UK and credit systems may vary if studying outside the UK. Within the UK you can sometimes transfer the credits obtained in one university to another course in another university, provided there is an overlap between subjects.

Some degree courses do not count the marks awarded in the first year towards your final degree classification, but will only count your assessed work in your second and third years. Do not feel this means you can take it easy in the first year though. If your work is not considered satisfactory you may not be allowed to progress to the second year.

Your degree result

Each student is awarded a degree classification at the end of their course, which is dependent on their performance throughout the degree and the marks they are awarded for each module.

A First Class degree is the best result you can get which indicates a lot of time, effort and a high standard of work.

A 2:1 or Upper Second is a good result showing a high standard of commitment and work and should enable students to progress to further study such as postgraduate study.

A 2:2 or Lower Second is an average degree classification. This might not set you apart from other students when you start to apply for jobs, especially with the expansion of higher education which has resulted in an increase in the number of graduates. If you are on line for a 2:2 try to ensure you have something extra or different to show employers when you are job hunting.

Third and Pass classifications are not a good result. Students who get Third Class or Pass degrees should have been aware that their performance was below standard and should have received feedback from their tutors stating this and advice on how to improve their work. Some students may have personal factors which affect their final result, such as relationship problems, illness or family issues.

A Fail needs little explanation.

Expectations of you

Most universities will provide you with details of your rights and responsibilities while you are a student. Be aware of your responsibilities and make sure you are familiar with the university's policies and procedures. You will be expected to:

- attend lectures, seminars and tutorials;
- meet deadlines set by your lecturers;
- participate in your learning by making a contribution;
- abide by the university regulations and policies.

Learning and teaching methods

A variety of methods will be used to help you learn about your subject area. Teaching methods are likely to vary from course to course depending on the subject. For example, art and drama students will take part in practical work in an art studio or theatre studio, science-based courses involve laboratory work and sport will involve activity in a gym or outdoor sports arena. Most degree courses will include lectures, seminars and tutorials as well as other teaching methods.

The teaching methods used in higher education are quite different to those used in school and any student whose last experience of study was many years ago in school will be surprised at the ways in which they will learn once they are in higher education.

Lectures

In a lecture an academic tutor or lecturer will present a talk on a particular topic related to the degree you are studying. The size of the lecture group will depend on how many students are on your course.

The lecturer will go over a lot of material and lectures should help students improve their listening and note-taking skills. It is sometimes difficult for students to get involved and it may be hard to ask questions and get feedback. Some students find large groups intimidating and it is important to have an environment without too many distractions and interruptions. To make the lecture really effective and interesting the lecturer needs good interpersonal and presentation skills.

To get the most out of a lecture prepare in advance and make sure you have done any required reading. Check the lecture venue in advance and turn up on time. If you are invited to ask questions then do so, but make sure you do not talk when the lecturer is talking.

Seminars

Seminars are smaller groups where students are normally given a topic or problem to discuss under the supervision of the tutor or lecturer. Students may need to do some research or reading in advance of the seminar as directed by the tutor and may be asked to present their work during the seminar. The seminar may relate to an earlier lecture and should build on subject knowledge.

Seminars involve students in debate and all students can ask questions and get feedback. Some, less confident, students find it difficult to contribute to discussions and therefore may find seminars daunting.

This can make it difficult to include all students and the tutor may then find it hard to assess all students' contributions if some do not participate. Seminars take time to facilitate and sometimes the debate can depart from the topic and lose focus.

Tutorials

Tutorials involve either small groups or individuals meeting a tutor to discuss some particular aspect of their work. They may hand in work, receive feedback on work already handed in or obtain guidance on a current assignment. It is important that students participate, ask questions and use the tutorial to raise any problems or queries.

The advantage of tutorials is that they can be flexible and arranged in relation to specific requirements. If they are held on a one to one basis with a tutor the student can discuss confidential issues, ask questions and get feedback. Tutorials have an important role in helping to motivate and enthuse students, but the opposite can also happen.

If the tutor/student relationship is not a good and trusting one neither student nor tutor will benefit. In addition, tutorials may take time and sometimes lose focus. From the tutor's point of view it can be difficult to make sure that all students have an equal opportunity to meet with them either in groups or on a one to one basis.

Practical work

This might involve sport activity in a gym, teaching a lesson in a school, laboratory work on a science course, or creation of design work in a technology studio. Some practical work may take place in a real work situation during a work placement where students learn through experience and relate theoretical aspects of their course to a practical situation. Other practical work may take place in the university.

Practical work encourages a sense of working in a team and develops use of initiative, critical thinking, communication skills and problem-solving skills.

However, practical work can be expensive, both for the university and the student, and needs an appropriate environment, for example an art studio or sports facilities. Health and safety issues need to be considered and it may be necessary for the tutor to have additional technical help to help set up and supervise the session.

Group discussions

These involve a group of individuals taking time to have a discussion about a particular topic or a problem. They may have been given the topic or problem in advance and be expected to prepare for the debate by doing some research and reading. All involved should participate in the discussion and work together as a group, even if they hold opposing views.

Discussions should develop listening and questioning skills as well as confidence in speaking out and being persuasive in putting forward a point of view. Students may be encouraged to develop innovative approaches to problems and this develops critical thinking skills.

The leader of the discussion needs to facilitate the discussion and encourage participation by all. However, discussions can be dominated by confident students and in some cases can get out of hand. Discussions can take a long time and it may be difficult to focus on the topic or problem.

Assignment

This is a piece of work, such as an essay, a report, a dissertation or a case study, relating to a topic given out in advance by the tutor. There should be a deadline for submission and guidelines on the structure of the piece of work. Sometimes students are allowed to choose a topic with the approval of their course tutor, as is the case with a dissertation. The assignment is likely to include elements of planning, research, reading and writing.

Assignments develop study skills and independent learning and help to build on the student's studying and subject knowledge. Students should know what is expected of them, and by when, so clear guidelines should be given. Tutors can provide feedback on the assignment which helps them assess progress, but should take care to provide feedback in a diplomatic and sensitive way.

Online learning or e-learning

More degree courses now include some type of online learning, (which is also sometimes called e-learning), and increasingly use information and communications technology (ICT) to help students study. This might include email, the Internet, computer conferencing, electronic resources and online discussion groups. Online learning allows students to study outside a university environment in a more flexible way, provided of course they have access to a computer and the Internet.

There are various ways in which online learning can be used, ranging from being able to access lecture notes on a website through to having access to what is called a 'virtual learning environment' which provides a gateway to all online learning within your university.

Online learning can only be successful if there are certain things in place:

- The student has access to a computer!
- The student can use a computer.
- The university has a good understanding of online learning and how it can be used to support learning.
- Everyone who uses the virtual learning environment, and this means academic staff as well as students, knows how to use it and how to make it work.

Online learning should not simply be a way of accessing lecture notes and preferably should not be the only way in which you learn. It should be used alongside other learning and teaching methods described in this chapter.

Work-based learning and work placements

These are a feature of many degree courses and are an invaluable way of applying theoretical skills to practical work situations. Many courses, such as medicine, occupational therapy, teaching, physiotherapy, social work and nursing, involve work placements and these form an integral part of the course. This type of learning not only develops practical work-related skills, but also develops teamwork and communication skills. Furthermore, students on a work placement may find it a good opportunity to network and plan for when they graduate from their course. Any work-based learning or work placement can only succeed if students receive adequate supervision and support in the work situation and if they, and their supervisor, are clear on their roles. Work placements require observation so the tutor needs to arrange a suitable time to visit the place of work.

Independent study

Degree courses encourage independent study and your lectures and seminars give you the building blocks of subject knowledge which you are expected to develop by doing reading, research and assignments in your own time. Recognize the importance of independent study when you are choosing your course and deciding whether to study full- or part-time. Make sure you are fully prepared for independent study.

What next?

This chapter has looked at why people choose to study in higher education, the range and types of degree courses available and how courses are structured. It has also described the range of learning and teaching methods used and the advantages and disadvantages of each.

You should now have a better understanding of what higher education is and how it works. The next chapter deals with student finance, a subject close to many students' hearts.

6

STUDENT FINANCE

This chapter will help you:

- understand the financial implications of full- and part-time degree study;
- become aware of the financial support available to mature students in higher education;
- understand the importance of budget management.

Money is proving to be the main area of concern for me. I should have saved up prior to taking the course.

(History degree student)

Introduction

Financing a degree is not an easy matter. This is the case for almost all students, whatever age they are, and is a cause of anxiety. The reality is that studying a degree course will affect your finances. Many mature students have to reduce their hours of work, or stop work altogether, while they study and this will obviously have an impact on their household income. Most students find they need to do part-time work while they study for their degree. The secret is getting the balance right so that your studies do not suffer and your income is at a level at which you manage to keep going and avoid getting into too much debt.

Some students get the balance right and some, unfortunately, do not. As with many other aspects of higher education the key is in planning and preparation in advance of your studies, being realistic and avoiding too many financial surprises once you start.

The good old days

Some years ago students received a grant when they studied for a degree, but those days are over and student loans replaced grants in 1998. Of course, the problem with a loan is that it has to be paid back at a later date and it can be easy to ignore a debt until it comes round to the time to repay it.

The university perspective

All degree courses have a cost implication and universities need funds to pay for their facilities, staff costs and other costs associated with running courses. Universities receive their funding from Higher Education Funding Councils and funding is dependent on the number of students they have on their courses.

How much?

It's important to do thorough research into financing your degree as part of your planning. Although the information given below is accurate at the time of writing, legislation relating to tuition fees, student loans and financial support changes frequently so it is best to get as much up to date information as possible.

Full-time study

Mature students choose full-time study for a variety of reasons. Many students want to complete their course quickly and some degree courses are not available to study part-time.

Tuition fees

Most degree courses charge tuition fees for each year of study although there are some exceptions to this, such as health and social care degree courses.

In the UK, before 2006 students were income assessed as to their ability to pay tuition fees and, if liable for part payment or full payment, had to pay this amount upfront at the beginning of each year of their degree course. Tuition fees were set at a standard amount for all universities.

In England from 2006 universities may choose to charge up to a maximum set figure each year in tuition fees (called top up fees), although they can opt to charge a lower figure if they wish. No student will have to pay fees before or while they study, but will be able to apply for a loan to cover tuition fees. Students will repay this loan once they have left university and start to earn over a certain amount.

Scottish students who study in Scotland do not pay tuition fees, but may have to pay back a graduate endowment at the end of the degree course. There are various income assessed loans and bursaries available for Scottish students regardless of whether they study in Scotland or elsewhere in the UK.

Welsh students who study in Wales may have to pay tuition fees up to a maximum set figure depending on their income. There are special grants for Welsh students who are studying in Wales.

Northern Ireland will operate top up tuition fees and a deferred repayment system such as that operated in England.

If you are a UK national and you choose to study outside your country of residence, in either England, Northern Ireland, Scotland or Wales, make sure you check which fee system will apply to you and do not assume you will come under the fee system in operation in that country.

Grants and bursaries

Full-time students on a low income may be eligible for a non-repayable grant each year, depending on their circumstances. This grant will be paid direct to the student each term. Some universities will also award bursaries to students who receive these grants or special bursaries according to particular circumstances. This means that, depending on the amount of grant and/or bursary received, some students will not be liable to pay any tuition fees and some students will pay a proportion of tuition fees.

Student loans

Full-time students are entitled to apply for a student loan for each year they study if they are aged under 55. If you are aged 50 to 54 you will need to show that you intend to work after the end of your course. This loan is to cover living costs, such as accommodation, food, bills and general expenses. There is a maximum loan amount available to take out each year, with a higher amount available for students in London. A percentage of the loan is dependent on your income. The student loan system is administered by the Student Loans Company.

Unfortunately, you must repay your student loan once you finish your course and start to earn over a certain set amount. Repayment is structured according to how much you earn and is deducted from your salary in instalments and the rate of interest on the loan is linked to the rate of inflation. If you become self-employed repayments will be collected through the tax self-assessment system. You can receive a student loan even if you have previously studied in higher education.

How to apply

Contact details for relevant organizations are listed in the section at the end of this book entitled 'How to get further advice'. These will be able to provide you with further guidance. You will need to apply early to determine your eligibility for grants, bursaries and student loans and provide details of your income if you are classed as an independent student or details of your parents' income if you are classed as dependent on your parents.

You will be classed as independent if you are 25 or over, you have been married before the start of the academic year, you have been living independently for three years, or you have no living parents. In some circumstances you are classed as independent if you are estranged from your parents.

All applicants for financial support will need to meet certain requirements regarding residency and immigration status.

International students

If you live outside the UK, and are considering studying in the UK, make sure you investigate the situation regarding tuition fees, grants, bursaries and loans.

Part-time study

The amount charged for part-time study, and the method of payment, varies from university to university. Some universities have special rates for the first few modules and then charge the usual rate once you have done a certain number of modules. Generally, you should find that you pay for your modules as you do them and in most places will be invoiced for the cost of the module. You might be allowed to pay in instalments so don't forget to ask if this is possible.

Part-time students in England, Wales and Northern Ireland, who are on a low income or on income assessed benefits, (such as Income Support, Jobseeker's Allowance, Housing Benefit and Council Tax Benefit), may be entitled to a fee grant and course grant to cover the cost of modules and general course costs. Part-time students in Scotland may qualify for a fee waiver and a means tested student loan. You might be expected to complete your studies in a specified amount of time in order to qualify for this sort of financial help. Your local education authority will assess your entitlement to the fee and course grant. Once the course starts part-time students can ask for help from the university's Access to Learning Fund and may also be able to claim Disabled Students' Allowances.

It is important to ask for help and advice about the costs of part-time study as financial support packages change from time to time.

Distance learning

Distance learning students may be able to claim the part-time fee grant and course grant as outlined above. Any other funding to follow a distance learning degree course is dependent on the institution offering the course. If you have decided to study for a distance learning degree check with the university you have applied to and find out if they offer any kind of financial assistance. The Open University, who offer a wide range of distance learning degrees, provide some grants for students who are on a low income in addition to the funding provided by the government.

Exemptions

You may find that there are some exemptions to obtaining financial support. This can sometimes be the case if you have undertaken previous study in higher education and received help from public funds. If you have previously studied in higher education, but had to withdraw for personal reasons, contact your local education authority for advice about whether you are entitled to apply for financial assistance this time round.

Special help available

Students with disabilities

Full-time and part-time students with disabilities may receive help with any extra costs associated with their course and their disability, such as specialist equipment, a non-medical helper's allowance, a general allowance or extra travel costs. These are called Disabled Students' Allowances and are not dependent on household income. To qualify for this financial support you will need to provide medical proof of your disability, or if you have a specific learning difficulty such as dyslexia you will need to provide evidence of this. Before you start your course make sure you investigate any additional support offered by your university.

Parents and childcare

You may get extra help if you have children and childcare commitments. There is a comprehensive range of grants and allowances available, but these can be difficult to understand. A non-repayable Childcare Grant is available for full-time students to cover the additional cost of childcare incurred while you study, but applies only to registered and approved childcare. There is also a non-repayable Parents' Learning Allowance, for full-time students, assessed on income. These grants and allowances are assessed via your local education authority. This kind of financial support may change from time to time and it is important to ask for help and advice about your entitlement and to do this as early on as possible.

Adult dependents

You might get additional help if you have an adult dependent who depends on you financially. This help will probably depend on your income and the income of your adult dependent. Make sure that any help you get will not affect any benefits payable to your adult dependent.

Teacher training

You may be entitled to a training salary if you are on a postgraduate course leading to qualified teacher status at primary or secondary level. There are other financial incentives, relating to subject specialisms, for students who wish to become secondary school teachers. These incentives can change each year so check with your chosen university to see what is available. The Training and Development Agency for Schools can provide help about financial incentives available if you train as a teacher.

National Health Service bursaries

These are available for full-time or part-time courses related to healthcare professions such as chiropody, dental hygiene, dietetics, nursing, midwifery, occupational therapy, physiotherapy, radiography and speech and language therapy (this list is not comprehensive). To obtain the bursary you must be accepted for an NHS funded place in a university. There is also financial assistance for medical and dental students in their fifth and further years of study. These bursaries will take into account your income and that of your dependents.

Social work bursaries

The General Social Care Council awards bursaries for students who are on approved social work degree or diploma courses. Contact the General Social Care Council for more information.

University funds

All universities in England have Access to Learning Funds provided by the government to help full- and part-time students who are struggling with their finances. These funds can cover financial hardship, emergency payments and some costs not met from other grants. They can also be used to help students who may be considering giving up their course because of financial problems. Students apply direct to the university to access these funds and will be asked to provide details of their income. Don't rule out these funds on the basis of being too proud to ask; they are provided specifically to help you continue on your course. Similar schemes operate in Northern Ireland, Scotland and Wales.

Travel costs

If you are doing a course such as medicine or dentistry, and you are undertaking clinical training on placement, you may receive help with travel costs to your placement. This help is usually assessed on your income. Some universities may also reimburse travel costs to work placements for degree courses such as occupational therapy and physiotherapy.

Career development loans

Students who can't get funding from the local education authority or from other means may be eligible to apply for a career development loan. These are primarily for vocational related courses and you will need to repay the loan once you finish your course. Application forms are available from the career development loan information line.

Professional studies loans schemes

These are operated through banks and apply to certain courses, such as medicine, law and architecture.

Educational charities and trusts

There are a number of educational trusts and charities. Some specifically provide help for people who are keen to further their education and training and some provide help to specific groups or people doing specific courses. You will probably need to write letters or complete application forms to claim funding and there is no guarantee of being successful in your claim. The trusts and charities probably receive requests from thousands of potential and current students. Further information can be found in publications such as the Educational Grants Directory or the Charities Digest, both of which should be available in your local library.

Sponsorship

Some students get sponsorship from employers, although this is often in the fields of business, science, engineering and the armed forces. These students will usually be expected to undertake a certain amount of work for that employer or even commit to working with the employer once they graduate. The amount of sponsorship can vary depending on the company and the course being followed. In some cases students may find that their current employer is prepared to cover some of their study costs so do not be afraid to ask.

Social security benefits

Some students, for example those with a disability or dependent children, may be able to receive benefits while they study. People in receipt of Jobseeker's Allowance may be able to receive financial help under the New Deal scheme. Check your entitlement with your local Job Centre Plus office.

What else?

Some students are exempt from council tax subject to certain conditions. If you are a full-time mature student and live in a household with a person who is not a student you may get a 25 per cent reduction on your council tax. You should be exempt from council tax if you live in a university hall of residence. You may also qualify for free dental and optical treatment if you are on a low income.

A word about debt

Some mature students start their studies in debt and may already have mortgages, existing credit card debt, rent arrears or loan repayments. This makes it even harder to juggle your finances as a student. Always take into account any current loans and debts you have when you are planning your return to study and consider whether you will be able to manage to continue repayments on these as well as coping with the financial constraints of being a student.

If debt is mounting to a worrying extent while you are studying make an appointment to speak to someone from a specialist agency as they can offer help, advice and support in arranging repayments. There are organizations, such as the Citizens' Advice Bureau and welfare rights advisers, who are able to provide specialist help if you are having severe financial difficulties.

Budgeting

You may now be thinking that higher education study is financially impossible but, despite the gloomy picture of student finance, many mature students do study (they form 25 per cent of the total full-time student population) and they manage financially because of careful planning, preparation and budgeting.

It won't always be easy financially, but it won't necessarily be impossible. If you feel unable to consider full-time study because of work commitments and the need to keep your income at a certain level, consider part-time study as an option. Don't forget that flexible and distance learning might be the answer if you are unable to reduce the hours you work. As a mature student, perhaps with family, mortgage, bills and work commitments you are probably used to budgeting and making your finances go a long way.

Budgeting before you start your course

List all the outgoings you cannot possibly avoid, such as mortgage, rent, bills, food and any credit or loan repayments. Calculate what income you need to enable you to keep on top of these costs and how many hours of work you will need to do to get that income. Then think carefully about whether you will be able to study full- or part-time.

If you have a collection of credit and store cards get rid of all of them. Their convenience can often tempt you into using them too frequently; they are high interest and usually charge a penalty for late payment. If you get into arrears with your credit or store cards you risk being added to a credit list and this will affect loan or mortgage applications in the future.

Make sure you sort out your tuition fee and student loan assessment early on in the year you wish to study. The earlier you start the more likely you will have your finances in order when you begin your course and your student loan will then be available when you need it most – at the beginning of term.

When you visit the university prior to starting your course speak to student finance advisers. Find out as much as you can about any extra financial help the university offers, such as special grants and bursaries. You will need to let them know your personal circumstances and give as much information as possible so they can identify appropriate financial support.

Case study

Surash made a decision to study part time and started halfway through the academic year. She had received no finance advice and was unsure of any financial support she would receive. Because of this she felt anxious and this was affecting her confidence. After several discussions with advisers she decided to withdraw from study and return as a full-time student in September, the beginning of the academic year. Advisers helped her claim financial support and she has now completed two years of study.

Be realistic about the costs of your course. Some practical based courses, such as art or sport, may incur extra costs for materials or sports kit, while others, such as Geography, involve field trips and you may be expected to cover accommodation costs. Teacher training and occupational therapy include work placements, which will involve daily travel and in some cases living in temporary accommodation. Be aware of your course commitments and find out whether any associated costs can be reclaimed from the university.

Don't underestimate other costs. All students will need to buy some academic text books and some books, such as science or medical books, can be more expensive than others. You will need money for photo-copying and printing, drinks and food while in university, travel to and from university, stationery and paying library fines (try to avoid these!).

Get a student bank account with interest free overdraft facilities. Take advantage of introductory offers, such as free CDs, vouchers or cash, provided by banks and building societies when you open your student account. Decide which is important to you, make a note of the bank charges and choose an account most suitable for you. Think about paying bills by direct debit as you can sometimes get discounts by paying this way. If you are moving to student accommodation make sure your possessions are covered by contents insurance and contact specialist student insurance companies. Do not forget to get a TV licence.

Speak to some current mature students and find out how they manage to budget. They will probably be able to share helpful in-formation with you and help you avoid some financial pitfalls. Current students are a valuable source of information as they are open and honest about their own experiences.

Budgeting while you study

Maintain a good relationship with your bank or building society and don't give them any surprises. If times get hard go and talk to them and ask them for help. This is better than ignoring the situation and thinking your problem will go away.

Get to know the student finance team in the university. They will be a valuable source of information, will help with budget management and keep you informed of any grants and bursaries. Financial support varies from year to year, so if you keep in contact with them you have more chance of finding out about new types of support.

Be prepared to take up a part-time job if you don't already have one. Very few students get through higher education without working part time, but be careful not to take on too many hours. It is recommended that students do no more than 15 hours of work per week as any more than this may affect your studies.

Find out if the university has a job bureau advertising jobs for students. If they do have one it is likely that the vacancies will be with employers who are used to employing students and will be prepared to be flexible with hours of work. Also check out any employment opportunities on the university campus. There may be bar or catering work available and this might fit in with your studies and be a more convenient location for work.

Some students, such as lone parents or disabled students, are entitled to benefits, such as Income Support, Housing Benefit, Child Tax Credit or Working Tax Credit. Discuss this with your student welfare adviser if you feel you may be entitled.

Be aware of your employment rights relating to conditions of employment. If you earn less than the taxable personal allowance ask your employer to complete an Inland Revenue form so you do not have tax deducted from your salary. If you are not sure about this get further advice from student welfare services, the students' union or the Citizens' Advice Bureau.

If you are a member of the students' union you will be entitled to get discounts in a variety of places such as shops, cinemas and pubs.

Share costs, such as travel and photocopying, with your fellow students. You might be able to share childcare responsibilities with them, but bear in mind that if you are receiving financial help for childcare you will probably be expected to use a registered childminder, rather than friends and family who may not be registered.

If you are a full-time student you should be entitled to a railcard, which will save you money on each rail journey you take. There is little point in getting one if you do not use rail travel frequently, but you can often save the cost of the railcard by making just one rail journey.

Don't feel you have to rush out and buy all the books on your reading lists from your tutors. Ask which ones they most recommend you buy and then use the university library to obtain the others. You could save money by buying secondhand textbooks from current students. However, you may need the latest version of a textbook if you are doing a course such as science or healthcare.

Don't feel afraid to ask for help if you are worried about your finances. You may feel you know all there is to know about budgeting, but even the most financially astute students struggle sometimes.

Try to have an emergency fund. It makes you feel safe, secure and less pressured.

(Foundation degree in rehabilitation student)

What next?

You should now have a realistic idea about student finance and how to ensure financial survival as a higher education student. Many mature students do survive their degree years even if they prove to be financially challenging. Be realistic, do some research into the support offered, ask questions and make sure you claim all you are entitled to.

The next chapter covers choosing a course and university and provides guidance on what to look for and how to decide which course and university is right for you.

7

CHOOSING A COURSE AND UNIVERSITY

This chapter will help you:

- understand the best ways of finding advice about degree courses and universities;
- identify factors to consider when choosing a course;
- identify factors to consider when choosing a university.

Introduction

Choosing a course and university can be complicated because there are around five hundred institutions in the UK offering over fifty thousand higher education courses. This chapter looks at factors to consider when choosing a course and a university.

Many mature students prefer to study locally rather than moving away to study. There might be a variety of reasons for this, such as having children in local schools, wanting to live close to family and friends, having a mortgage or not wishing to leave their place of work. Therefore, the options open to mature students who do not wish to relocate are restricted to universities within travelling distance of where they live. Consider distance learning as an option if you feel your choice locally is limited.

This won't be the case for all mature students though and some will move away to study and might have to do so if their chosen course is not available locally. Moving away to study is a major decision and should involve a lot of careful planning and preparation.

Where to start

Reflect back on your motivation for study. Why are you considering doing a degree?

You may wish to study for leisure or interest and therefore are not motivated by the need for a new job or career. Planning for your return to study will not need to include getting careers and employment advice.

Alternatively, you might be motivated by a desire for a new job or career and either be very focused on the course and career you've chosen or may not be sure what you want to do. Either way you should think carefully about your skills and future employment prospects and, above all, be realistic about your options.

If you are unsure try to have some idea of subjects you definitely do not want to study and reflect on work you have done and enjoyed and skills you use now and have used in the past. Then try consulting local advice and guidance organizations before starting to investigate courses and universities. There are a variety of organizations providing advice, some of it free of charge, and you might benefit from a one to one interview to help you plan your future.

Most areas have a local careers advice centre which contains a careers resource library with information about different types of jobs and careers and the types of qualifications needed. If you are unsure where your local careers centre is contact your local Citizens' Advice Bureau for advice.

Be aware that there may be a number of routes to your preferred job and always take advice just in case there are options other than a degree course.

How to find out about courses and universities

Universities and Colleges Admissions Service (UCAS)

UCAS is the organization which coordinates applications for full-time degrees and has a comprehensive website (www.ucas.com) detailing all full-time degree courses where you can search by subject and by region. It also produces printed guides, which should be available in your local careers centre or public library.

In addition, UCAS holds regional higher education conventions during the year, at which around one hundred and fifty universities attend. This is a good opportunity for students to find out more about different universities by attending one event. Although this is more relevant to students who intend to move away from home and apply to more than one university, it can also be valuable for mature students as a way of finding out more about courses and universities.

University literature and website

All universities publish a prospectus, course leaflets and other literature and all should have a website. The prospectus is a comprehensive listing of all their courses and also contains information about the university, such as the support they offer and the university's location. There may also be separate course leaflets, which outline the content of each degree course in more detail, and some universities have specific mature student guides. Treat university literature carefully as it is an increasingly glossy marketing tool and will show the university in a very good light with lots of positive comments from current and past students. Use literature to find out factual information about the university, the course you are interested in, how you apply for it and what entry qualifications you need. Use the university website in the same way, for factual information. Remember that expensive packaging does not always indicate a good product.

University open days and visits

These are held throughout the year, usually in the summer and autumn. Don't underestimate the importance of open days as they provide an opportunity to visit a university and find out more about it and its courses, meet staff and talk to current students. This is a vital part of your planning and preparation and although visiting universities takes time it is time well spent. Before you visit make a list of questions you need to ask, bearing in mind the factors which are going to affect your decision making. For example, if clubs and societies are important to you ask to speak to someone from the students' union. If you are more concerned about graduate employment ask a member of academic staff about the percentage of graduates who gain relevant employment.

Most universities should be able to accommodate you if you want to visit them again after an open day or you are unable to get to an open day. Some universities organize campus tours throughout the year guided by their students.

Quality and reputation

All universities are subject to inspection and review to make sure that the quality of their courses and teaching is up to standard. There are a number of ways in which you can check quality and reputation.

The Quality Assurance Agency for Higher Education (QAA at www.qaa.ac.uk) produces reviews on individual universities which highlight strengths and areas for improvement. The Research Assessment Exercise rates the quality of research in universities and awards research funding accordingly.

The Teaching Quality Information website (TQI at www.tqi.ac.uk) provides access to statistics and reports, related to individual universities, about the types of students on their courses, the completion rates (the number of students who finish a course) and the degree results obtained by their students. The results of student surveys should also be available on the TQI website.

The Higher Education Statistics Agency (HESA at www.hesa.ac.uk) publishes performance indicators relating to access to higher education, dropout rates (how many students leave their course early) and graduate employment. HESA emphasize that these are not league tables and should not be used as such. The Higher Education Funding Councils produce quite detailed information on the social mix in different universities and student completion and employment (www.hefce.ac.uk in England).

In addition, some newspapers publish league tables which rate teaching quality, research output, graduate employment, student/staff ratios, A level points of entrants, applications for places, dropout rates and how many students entered via clearing (this might indicate a university has a problem filling places on its courses). Universities have their own statistics on dropout rates, final degree results and the amount of their students who enter relevant employment after graduating. You should be able to get statistics relating to the particular course or courses you are interested in.

League tables, statistics and reviews can tell you quite a lot about universities and whether they are particularly respected in some subject areas or have a good research record. If you intend to enter a competitive profession, such as law or medicine, the awarding university may be important to a prospective employer. However, treat league tables, statistics and reviews with caution as the criteria used to compile them differs in each one. Do not use them as the main deciding factor in making your choice and always use the information you find in conjunction with other factors important to you. If you really like a university, its course and its staff don't be put off if it appears lower down on a league table than other universities.

Current mature students

Current mature students are generally open about their experiences and happy to advise prospective mature students. Their advice is useful as they can outline how they made decisions relating to course choice and how they manage their finances. Many will probably share any mistakes they made in their planning and preparation. More importantly, they provide a realistic picture of studying a degree as a mature student.

Bear in mind that those students who are around during open days to help and advise prospective students will probably be paid by the university to work on these events and will therefore be handpicked, enthusiastic and happy. It is highly unlikely that any university will ask unhappy students to work for them!

Some universities may put you in touch with current students or may have an online discussion forum where you can communicate with current students and ask questions as you progress through your planning and preparation. Some university websites may contain case studies of current students.

Seek the advice of others who have gone before you. They will have learned from their mistakes.

(Foundation degree in rehabilitation student)

Books and guides

There are a variety of books and guides about degree courses and universities. Some are more suitable for school leavers so may not contain information you find relevant and some are specifically for mature students. Browse through some of these books and guides as they do provide help for prospective students.

The customer

Remember you are a customer. Higher education is a business and each university has to ensure they receive enough applications to fill their student places and therefore get sufficient funding. Some universities find this easier to do than others and you will face competition for a place on some courses in some universities. Other universities do not face the same competition for places, but this does not necessarily mean they are less reputable or less able.

Course choice – what's available?

The simple answer is almost everything! The choice of subjects is vast and if you wish to you can study a degree in embroidery, fishing, golf course management, science fiction or fire science as well as more traditional subjects such as English, history, politics or classics.

The range of subjects on offer increases each year and, on the face of it, provides a wide range of options for prospective students. However, most students will not start their search for a course by working through those beginning with A (American studies) and ending with those beginning with Z (zoology). There will be many factors influencing how you choose the course you want to study.

Your skills

In Chapters 1 and 3 you were asked to reflect on your skills and how you have used them in your work and life experience. If you came to a conclusion about what you feel you are good at, and not so good at, relate this to particular courses. If you find it hard to empathize with people who are ill it would probably not be a good idea to choose nursing or occupational therapy. If you find children really annoying don't try to become a teacher. If you simply cannot understand maths don't try to become an engineer.

I was made redundant for the third time and started looking for a new direction. I had always enjoyed teaching apprentices a trade and colleagues suggested I try teaching at secondary level in schools.

(Design and technology degree student)

Your career goals

You might have a particular future career in mind and your choice of degree will be guided by these goals. For example, if you want to teach in a primary or secondary school it is advisable to take either a specific degree which combines subject knowledge and teaching placements or do a degree in a National Curriculum subject such as history, mathematics, art, sport, geography or English. If you want to be a nurse you need to do a nursing degree and if you wish to be an occupational therapist do a degree in occupational therapy. Some people are very focused on their future plans and the process of choosing a course is therefore easier in some ways, but may become problematic if they are unable to find this course locally and do not wish to move away to study.

Remember to be realistic about your career goals. If you intend to look for a particular job locally once you finish your course, try to find out more about the opportunities for those jobs in the area you live in. Check the local papers for job advertisements relating to the job you want to do and gain an idea of opportunities over a period of time. Speak to people who are doing the job you want to do and find out what they feel about opportunities for employment. Contact your local council to see if they have figures on local employment and current trends in local employment. Consider how far you are prepared to travel to get the job you want to do. You may need to reconsider your future plans if you are limited in the distance you can travel to work.

I decided to 'start again' and my desire to be a primary school teacher was nurtured by being involved in my children's schools. I chose history because it was my favourite subject at school and I was able to do an essay to support my application onto a degree programme.

(History degree graduate)

Professional requirements

Some careers have particular requirements regarding qualifications of people who wish to enter that profession. For this reason some degree courses are accredited by professional bodies so that (successful) students can enter that profession and gain membership of the professional body. For example, if you wish to become a chartered psychologist you need to do a psychology degree accredited by the British Psychological Society. Other professional bodies include the General Medical Council, the Engineering Council and The Royal Institute of British Architects. Any statutory or professional requirements may affect your course choice so get some further advice from a careers service, or the professional body, if you have a particular career in mind.

Entry requirements

University literature will indicate what entry qualifications and UCAS tariff points are needed for particular courses. The UCAS tariff gives points for different qualifications and a specific number will be needed for each course. If you do not have these qualifications or points, and you still want to do the course, you will need to gain the relevant entry qualifications. Some universities have special entry requirements for mature students who do not have formal entry qualifications. This might seem encouraging, but be careful as it is important you are prepared for higher education study. Be realistic and build any required entry qualification into your planning. Chapter 8 covers entry qualifications for degree courses in more detail.

Applications per place ratio

Some degree courses in some subjects are oversubscribed and you need to find out how many applications per place the university receives for the course or courses you are interested in. If they receive hundreds of applications for a small number of places make sure you have a back-up course and back-up university if possible. You may find oversubscribed courses do not make as many concessions for mature students without formal entry qualifications. If the course you are interested in applying for is a popular one you would be wise to make sure you fully satisfy the entry requirements before applying.

Employment prospects once you graduate

Be wary of glossy statistics published in university literature. You may be told that 85 per cent of students enter employment after graduating, but bear in mind that this might include graduates who are working in shops, bars or hotels. Ask how many students on the course you are interested in have got employment relevant to the course they have completed or are in graduate jobs. If you have a particular career in mind this is a very important question.

Work experience

You may have some work experience which you enjoyed and wish to build on. Think about different work environments you have been in, which ones you enjoyed and whether you can relate these to any particular course. Many degree courses have work experience built into the course and this can be invaluable when it comes to job hunting once you graduate.

Enthusiasm for the subject

If you have a real interest in a subject this is an excellent reason to study it at degree level. It is not a good idea to study a subject in which you only have a slight interest as you will find it difficult to keep motivated. An enthusiasm for the subject really keeps you going and if studying that subject helps you get a better job, or a job you really want to do, then all the better. If you find two or more subjects of interest find out if you can study them as a joint or combined or multi-disciplinary degree. Make sure the course covers areas of interest and relevance to you as there can be quite a difference in course content in different universities even if the subject appears the same.

Type of course

Chapter 5 outlined different types of course offered by higher education institutions and how they vary. Think about what type of course you want to do, for example a Higher National Diploma, a degree or a foundation degree. You might want to undertake relevant work experience or have the opportunity to study abroad. You may be more inclined towards part-time study because of time and financial commitments and will need to find out which courses can be studied part-time.

Teaching methods

It is important to find out how you will be taught on a degree course. Students will be expected to attend lectures, seminars and tutorials and be independent learners. There should be a variety of teaching methods used to accommodate students with different learning styles and if the teaching methods are limited they may not suit your way of learning. Part of your planning should involve asking university staff to give you an overview of a typical student week, how you will be taught and how many hours you will be expected to spend in university.

Academic support

You will find it useful to ask about the ratio of academic staff to students and do some comparisons between the courses you are interested in. Universities with fewer academic staff and high student numbers may only be able to offer large group lectures and fewer tutorials, and you may have more difficulty in getting help while you study. All students should be allocated an academic tutor and it would be useful to find out in advance how often you will be able to see your tutor and exactly what support they offer. This might differ from department to department in the same university. Academic staff should ideally have postgraduate qualifications such as a Masters degree or a Doctorate.

Assessment methods

Whether you like it or not you will have assignments to do and these will test your subject knowledge and let your tutors know how you are progressing with your studies. Universities use a variety of ways to assess students, such as essays, reports, group or individual presentations, work placements, observations, practical work and exams. Ask about the assessment methods used on the courses you are interested in.

Student support

If you have specific support requirements and you think that aspects of some courses may prove difficult, such as field trips or practical work, ask the university whether they will provide extra support or take your particular requirements into account. It is important to do this before you start to apply.

Other mature students

You might want to know how many mature students are on the course you are interested in, possibly because you feel anxious about being the only mature student amongst younger ones. It may be an important factor in making your decision, but should not be the most important one. If there are few mature students on the course it doesn't mean you will find it difficult to fit in or you will feel isolated. Decide how much you want to do that particular course and how much it fits in with your future plans. Many universities have mature student societies so you will meet other mature students even if there are not many on your course. Compare it to starting a new job in a new organization; you can't always guarantee there will be people like you working there.

> Talking with other students I was soon to discover the way I felt was shared by the majority of them, and being mature did not matter as I found we were all in the same boat.
>
> (Design and technology degree student)

Flexibility of course

Find out if the university is used to mature students, if the lecture timetable takes into account childcare commitments and if they will understand the demands of combining family and work commitments with degree level study.

University choice

It is important to make sure the university is the right one for you and one in which you feel comfortable. It helps to consider the following points when making your decision.

Local or far away

This is probably the most important decision you need to make. Many mature students study locally for a variety of reasons and are in a different position from that of school leavers who are probably more able to move away from home. If you have to study locally you may have a choice of one or two universities within travelling distance.

If you have a specific course in mind for a particular career, and the course is not offered locally, you must decide if your reasons for doing the course are sufficient justification to make a move. This can be easier if you have no dependents, but will still involve a significant change in your life. This is an important decision and really needs to be talked over with family and friends before you make up your mind.

You will also need to decide whether you prefer a university in a city or a town and compare this to what you are used to and where you will feel most at home. You will have access to more facilities, such as restaurants, theatres and leisure centres in a city, but will probably be on a tight budget so may not have the opportunity to enjoy these facilities.

What type?

There are a variety of higher education institutions ranging from universities to colleges of higher education to colleges of further education and the Open University and all offer degree courses. The range of courses offered, the atmosphere and size of institution will vary considerably from place to place.

These institutions vary in size and you need to decide which environment you will feel comfortable in. For example, the University of Leeds has over 31,000 students, the University of Wales Lampeter has almost 2000 students and The Open University has over 150,000 students throughout the UK. Some students prefer a large university environment whereas other students may find this too daunting, especially if they haven't studied for some time and feel anxious about returning to study anyway.

It is important to get a feel for the university or universities you are interested in by visiting them before you apply and before you start your course.

Support services

All universities have a range of support services to support their students while they study. These might include mature student advisers, finance advisers, counselling staff, faith advisers, careers advisers, welfare networks, disability support and writing support. If you have particular support needs, a disability for example, most universities should be able to offer you support, but its quality and range will differ from place to place. The best way to find out is to ask for information about the services universities offer and try to speak to a current student to get the real picture. If you do need extra support you should be honest and open about your needs to ensure that you get all you are entitled to. Chapter 10 outlines these services in more detail.

Childcare

This is an important consideration for many mature students and you may wish to investigate the type and quality of childcare provision at the universities you are visiting. This will be particularly important if you intend to move away from home. Many universities offer childcare facilities on site and some of these facilities, even if they are privately owned and run, may offer subsidies to students' children. Places are likely to be in short supply and it is probably best to book a place for your child as early as possible, once you have decided where you want to study. If you intend to study locally you may already have organized childcare or have family or friends who help you out.

Facilities

If you want to do a practical based course such as sport or science or nursing make sure the university has appropriate and up to date facilities and equipment relevant to the course. Try to find out how much money has been invested in these facilities over the last few years and generally how much has been invested in the university. Ask if the equipment you need is all on one site or whether you will have to travel to another site for some of your lectures.

Multi-site campus

Some universities have more than one campus and it is always worth finding out which campus you will be based at as this could make a difference to your travel costs and time spent travelling. If there is more than one campus ask whether there are any plans for the future to either expand or close down. Some universities have closed their smaller sites to save funds and use these to invest in other facilities. It can be disconcerting to start your studies on one campus and then find you have to move to another campus halfway through your course.

Other mature students

If this is important to you find out how many mature students are in the university you are interested in attending. Some have a higher percentage of mature students than others and this may indicate they are used to dealing with particular issues relating to mature students. Find out if there they have societies for mature students to help you meet people and integrate into university life.

Atmosphere

Visit the university at an open day. These are held by all universities frequently throughout the year and are an excellent opportunity to look around the campus, meet academic staff, find out more about the courses and generally get a feel for the place. If you feel comfortable at an open day and you find the university warm and welcoming this is a good sign. Bear in mind that open days are a marketing tool and all staff will be on their best behaviour!

Accommodation

If you intend to move away from home and live in university accommodation make sure you have the opportunity to look around the accommodation beforehand. You may have the opportunity to do this at an open day. The standard of accommodation will vary considerably from place to place and the price may range from £50 to £100 per week, depending on whether you choose catered or self-catering accommodation. Some universities have houses where students live with about four or five other students and you might find there is specific accommodation for mature students. If there is no specific accommodation think about how you will feel living with groups of younger students.

Library resources

University libraries, or learning resource centres, should have a range of online and electronic resources available to students as well as books, journals and newspapers and adequate provision of computers for students to use. When you visit a university ask for a tour of the library or learning resource centre and find out about opening hours. Speak to current students about the library, but bear in mind that when they tell you that there are not enough copies of books then this will be the case in most universities as the library budget is generally never large enough to cater for all.

Faith and beliefs

You might hold strong opinions on faith and this may influence your choice of university. Find out more about the culture of the university by looking at the prospectus or website. Ask if there are any particular student societies catering for your faith or belief.

Social activities

Find out what the university social life is like and if clubs, societies and sporting activities are important to you ask for information on what is available.

What next?

This chapter has described the ways in which you can find out information about courses and universities. It has outlined some of the factors to consider when choosing a course and a university. Make a checklist to help you when you visit universities and prepare questions in advance to ensure you get all the information you need when you visit.

The next chapter describes courses which specifically prepare you for higher education study.

8

PREPARATION COURSES FOR HIGHER EDUCATION

This chapter will help you:

- understand the range of qualifications and courses which help you progress to higher education;
- understand how to apply for a higher education degree course;
- prepare a personal statement as part of your application;
- prepare for an interview.

Introduction

You should now have some idea about the course you want to do and the university or universities you wish to apply to. You should also have an understanding of the study skills needed to ensure your degree study is a success. If you have had a look at university literature and attended an open day you will also be aware of the qualifications and preparation needed prior to applying to do a degree.

If you haven't studied for some time and have few formal qualifications, such as O levels, GCSEs or A levels, it is advisable to spend time studying and gaining a qualification before applying to do your degree. Many universities like their applicants to demonstrate suitability for a degree through a range of qualifications, experience relevant to the course you want to do or by doing a study skills course.

Always bear in mind that whatever preparation you do, and however successfully you do it, you will not automatically get a place on your chosen degree course. You may have to satisfy further requirements by, for example, attending an interview or showing a portfolio of your work. The course you are applying for may be a very popular one, and competition for places may be high, so you could have all the right attributes and qualifications, but possibly still not get a place.

However, by obtaining an appropriate qualification, such as those outlined in this chapter, you gain a further set of skills and this should help to strengthen your application for a degree course.

Accreditation

There are a wide range of courses available which prepare students for degree courses. Many of these courses are accredited which means that if you complete your course work successfully and attend your classes you should leave with a qualification and will receive a certificate. Accreditation will be at a particular level and demonstrates your ability to study at that level and indicates the depth of study you have achieved. The courses listed below provide accreditation and are nationally recognized. Universities should recognize what the qualification is and understand the level at which you studied.

Universities and Colleges Admissions Service (UCAS) tariff

The UCAS tariff is a points system which allocates points to qualifications depending on the level of that qualification. Each degree course requires a particular number of tariff points as an entry requirement and universities specify this information in their literature. You may have a variety of qualifications which help you achieve the tariff points specified or may need to acquire qualifications to gain the points required. Many universities offer special entry for mature students so use the UCAS tariff as a guide and make sure you know if there are other flexible routes to the course you want to do.

Preparatory courses for higher education

General Certificate of Secondary Education (GCSE)

You may have done GCSEs (or O Levels) at school. Most universities will specify that applicants should have five GCSEs including Mathematics and English, but some may operate flexible entry conditions for mature students who have experience relevant to the course, but no GCSEs. Entry requirements vary from place to place so check out the requirement in the university you wish to apply to.

If you need to do some GCSEs don't worry too much or feel that you may be the only mature student doing them. There will probably be a range of GCSEs taught locally in adult education centres and colleges of further education. Many of these classes have mature students in them and the tutors should be experienced in teaching mature students.

Advanced Levels (A Levels)

A Levels are available at a range of venues, not just secondary schools, but also at adult education centres and colleges of further education. They usually take two years to complete and are available in a wide range of subjects, some of which are more vocational than others.

A Levels help you prepare for your degree course as they involve reading, writing essays, meeting deadlines and debating topics relevant to the subject. It does help to have an A Level related to the subject you are hoping to do at degree level as this will provide you with subject knowledge.

Most universities ask for a minimum of two A Levels, but may accept other equivalent qualifications instead. Some degree courses will be very specific about the subjects you have studied, for example science or language degrees, and may want a specific qualification in that subject area before they consider your application.

Don't worry if you have not had the opportunity to study A Levels before. Many mature students have not got A Levels, but are still doing degree courses because they have some experience relevant to their course or because they have demonstrated their competence to do a degree in another way. If you do not have the time or money to do an A Level ask the university whether there is an opportunity to apply for a degree without this qualification and what else they may take into account to support your application. Consider doing an Access course (see below).

Scottish and Irish Highers

In Scotland school pupils aged 16 to 18 years old undertake Highers or Advanced Highers which are equivalent to A Levels. These are accepted in universities in England and Wales and A Levels are accepted in universities in Scotland. Pupils in Ireland take the Irish Leaving Certificate, usually at age 17.

Access to higher education courses

Access to higher education courses are usually offered at further education colleges and are for mature learners, over the age of 19, who wish to access degree courses. They can be done full- or part-time, but this option will vary depending on the college and some colleges have evening and daytime provision. All providers of Access courses should acknowledge that their students are likely to have family or work commitments and the study timetable should reflect this.

Access courses prepare students for degree level study, provide valuable subject knowledge and help improve students' confidence in their ability to study. Most Access courses include elements of literacy, numeracy and IT skills and will be composed of units of study. If you successfully complete assignments for each unit you build up credits as you progress through the course and then receive a certificate for a successfully completed Access course. It is important to have a high percentage of level 3 units in the Access course as these prepare you for degree level study.

Courses on offer often relate to different subject pathways, for example there are pathways relating to teaching, healthcare, management studies and science. There are also general Access courses with no specified pathway.

If you decide to do an Access course choose your pathway carefully and ensure the subject relates to the degree you are eventually going to apply for. It helps to discuss your future plans and preferred degree course with the tutor in charge of Access courses. They will be able to advise on the right pathway to take and provide information about course commitments, timetable and methods of study.

Access courses should be accepted as a qualification to support your application to most universities. Check this with the university you are interested in applying to and find out how they view an Access course and what proportion of level 3 units they require.

> The Access course was tough. However, I thoroughly enjoyed the hard work and rewards it brought with it in terms of personal fulfilment and the satisfaction of knowing that I wasn't stupid just because I left school with few qualifications.
> (English literature and women's studies degree graduate)

BTEC National Diploma, National Certificate and National Award

BTECs are considered appropriate for progression to a degree course and are equivalent to A Level study. You will receive a certain amount of UCAS tariff points depending on whether you do the Diploma, Certificate or National Award. Before starting a BTEC make sure it is considered appropriate by the university you intend to apply to.

Higher National Diplomas (HNDs)

HNDs usually require two years of full-time study and are vocational in subject areas such as art and design or business studies. They are well regarded as a qualification in their own right or as a route to a degree course. It may be possible to enter the second year of a degree course if you have successfully completed an HND in a subject relevant to the degree. Check with your university of choice and find out if doing an HND will enhance your application and enable you to fast track into the second year of the degree.

Foundation year programmes

Some universities offer foundation programmes to enable students with ability, but without appropriate formal qualifications, to access higher education. Students usually do a foundation year and then, on successful completion, can progress onto a degree course in the same university.

Vocational qualifications

There are a range of vocational qualifications which are considered suitable for progression to a degree course. These include National Vocational Qualifications (NVQs) at level 3, which is equivalent to A Level, and might be considered suitable for higher education entry at some universities. These qualifications are related to particular job areas, are usually studied while working and assess competence at that job. Check with the university to find out if they accept these as an entry qualification for their degrees.

Statutory requirements for some courses

Even if universities are flexible about mature student entry onto their courses there are times when they must take into account statutory requirements laid down by professional organizations. For example, some degree courses in primary or secondary teaching require students to have mathematics and English GCSEs and, if you were born after 1 September 1979, a science GCSE before applying. Find out if there are any statutory requirements relating to your preferred course, as you will have to satisfy these before gaining a place.

Previous higher education study

If you have studied at degree level before you may find you can transfer any credits gained to a new degree course in another university. This depends on the level of credit gained and how the subject you previously studied maps onto the subject you want to study. If you are going to study a completely different subject you may find that your credits are accepted for entry purposes, but that you cannot use them to gain credit against the new subject.

Open University courses

There are a range of Open University courses, offered by distance learning, which help adults who haven't studied for some time. 'Openings' courses relate to various subject areas and help improve study skills. The Open University also does a range of other courses at different levels, and of different durations, which help students progress to degree level study either with them or elsewhere.

Modern apprenticeships

These involve learning while working and are therefore vocationally based in that they relate to particular jobs. Do not do a modern apprenticeship as preparation for higher education unless you are sure the university you are interested in accepts them as an entry level qualification.

Baccalaureate qualifications

These qualifications are usually taken by school pupils aged 16 to 18 years old. There are different types of Baccalaureate and most involve taking a range of subjects at different levels. The International Baccalaureate Diploma may be acceptable for higher education entry, but the Certificate may not be. Check with the university to find out if they accept these as an entry qualification for their degrees.

Other ways to prepare for higher education

Return to learn courses

You should be able to find a range of these in adult education centres, colleges of further education and in some universities. Not all will be accredited in that you may receive a certificate of attendance for some, but not necessarily a standardized qualification recognized by all universities. However, these courses are always useful, whether accredited or not, as they help you return to study and build up confidence. They can be an excellent starting point if you have not studied for some time.

Case study

'With two small children I decided to brush up on my basic skills. To be honest, it was more about helping with homework than any real aspiration to do something for me, but it got the ball rolling. It was great! I started doing a "help your child with Key Stage 2 maths" course which was a perfect beginning. I could hide behind the idea I was doing it to just help my kids, but really I was doing it as I was too scared to go to a college being older than the standard students. After that I did a similar English course, then first aid and then a counselling course. I was then ready to do an Access in the Community course, and am currently at university! It was an incredible way to get back into education.'

(Drama degree student)

Mature student entry to degree courses

Some universities have different entry requirements for mature students and recognize the fact that, if you have few or no formal qualifications, you have probably got skills from work and life experience. They may ask you to do a short essay relating to the subject you wish to study or ask you to an interview. Do not be disappointed if the university decides you are not yet ready for degree level study. It is better to know this in advance rather than find out once you have started a degree. Ask for advice about how you can be better prepared and what type of preparatory course would help.

Work experience

Do not underestimate the value of work experience, especially if it relates to the degree subject you want to study. There are many vocational degree courses related to specific jobs or work environments. If you wish to apply for one of these, and your work experience is directly relevant, make the most of this in your application as this may be more important to the university than having formal qualifications. Current work experience in a relevant setting may be an entry requirement for some courses such as foundation degrees. If your work experience is not relevant to the subject you wish to study reflect on the transferable skills gained, for example, communication skills, teamwork, problem solving and decision making. Mature students have an advantage here as almost all have some experience of working, perhaps in a variety of jobs.

Workplace visits and observations

Some universities advise applicants to find out more about particular jobs before they apply, especially if the degree course relates to a specific area of work. For instance, if you want to do an occupational therapy degree try and arrange a visit to a local hospital to find out more about the job and speak to an occupational therapist. If you are interested in teaching try to spend some time working in a school. This shows commitment on your part and indicates you have an overall view of the job and what it involves.

Accreditation of Prior Experiential Learning (APEL)

APEL provides a way of accrediting experience for mature students who may not have formal qualification such as A Levels or an Access qualification. The APEL process is a way of looking at your achievements in life (for example doing voluntary work, running a home, child-minding) and giving them a value, which is then used to support your application for a degree. Universities using APEL usually ask for a portfolio detailing your experience and what you learned from it and this can sometimes be a complicated way of valuing experience. Find out from the university if they operate an APEL system.

Computer courses

You may need to consider upgrading your computer skills if you want to do a degree as most universities will want you to word-process your work. There should be a wide range of computer courses available in your locality, in adult education centres, colleges of further education or LearnDirect centres. If you are a newcomer to computer skills start with a few short workshops and then progress onto an accredited course, such as the European Computer Driving Licence. Try not to start your degree course with little or no background knowledge of computer skills as you will find that once you start the course you have to get to grips with this as well as the subject of the degree itself.

> Although I had taken a computer course, on reflection I would have done other computer courses as even now I do not feel particularly confident with my computer skills. Very specific things like setting out essays, sending emails with attachments, etc.
> (Theatre, film and television degree student)

Study skills

Chapter 4 covered a range of study skills relating to study at higher education. If you undertake any preparatory course you are likely to improve your study skills as you do so. This will help you when you study your degree.

Transferable skills

Do not underestimate the transferable skills gained from life and work experience. Look back at Chapters 1 and 3 and relate these skills to studying. You should be able to describe these skills in the application form for the degree course and in an interview if you are required to have one.

How to apply

Full-time study

The Universities and Colleges Admissions Service (UCAS) is an organization which coordinates applications for full-time degree study and handles approximately two million applications from around 450,000 applicants each year. There is a UCAS application form and guidance notes and a 'Mature students' guide to higher education' to help applicants.

You can complete the application form either online or on paper. For some courses, such as medicine, dentistry and veterinary science and those at Oxford and Cambridge, you need to submit your application form to UCAS by 15 October of the year before you intend to study. All other applications should be with UCAS by 15 January of the year in which you intend to study. It is advisable to try and keep to this deadline, especially if the degree course you want to do is popular. However, many mature students do apply for degree courses later on, sometimes right up to a couple of weeks before the start of the course. It is best to avoid this if possible as you have less planning time the later you apply.

The UCAS application form asks for factual information such as your personal details, information about the courses and universities you are interested in applying for, any special support requirements, details of qualifications already obtained and details of qualifications for which you are awaiting results. It is important to follow the UCAS guidelines for completing the form.

You can apply for up to six degree courses in more than one university, but it may look odd if you apply for very different subjects at one university. You would have to justify why you are doing this and why your interests are varied.

The most important part of the UCAS form is the personal statement. You need to promote yourself and include information which identifies you as an individual and which is relevant to the course you are applying for. It is important to do a draft or drafts before doing the final statement so take a photocopy of the UCAS form and practise on this. Some universities offer help with completing the UCAS form or may look at your rough draft for you and make suggestions.

Try to include the following in your personal statement:

- why you have chosen the subject and what interests you about it;
- why you have decided to change direction and do a degree course as a mature student;
- your career plans or an indication that you are keeping your options open;
- your work or life experience and how this relates to the degree course;
- what experience of responsibility you have had, such as management or supervision;
- what transferable skills and personal qualities you have and how these can help you do the degree course;
- what you have done to help you progress to the degree, e.g. study skills courses, evening classes, visiting colleges on open days, talking

to employers to find out more about the job you are interested in, etc.;

- your leisure interests and whether you belong to any voluntary, community or social groups;

Remember:

- If you are applying to one particular subject area make your personal statement directly relevant.
- Use action words such as 'discovered', 'reviewed' and 'demonstrated' when describing your experiences.
- Do not be tempted to exaggerate the truth!

You need to provide a reference, preferably someone who can comment on your academic ability and readiness for study. If you are doing a preparatory course ask your tutor if they will provide a reference. They have probably done so for other students in the past so should be aware of the importance of it and what they need to comment on, such as your suitability, potential, motivation and commitment. If you are not currently doing a course, and have not done so for a number of years, an employer would be a good choice for a referee. Alternatively you might ask someone who knows you well, for example a professional such as your GP or a careers officer. Do not ask your family or friends for a reference as this will not be accepted.

Once the application form is complete send it to UCAS and keep a photocopy for reference. You will need to pay a fee as indicated on the form. Your application will be acknowledged by UCAS and you can monitor the status of your application on their website. UCAS will send a photocopy of your application form to the universities listed on your form.

Once the form is received at the university their admissions staff will go through it, looking for applicants who they feel are ready for higher education, who will contribute and who will get the most out of degree study. When admissions and academic staff have made a decision they will inform UCAS who will let you know whether you have an offer of a place. If you do get an offer it will be one of the following:

- an unconditional offer, which means you have been accepted without having to satisfy any further requirements;
- a conditional offer, which means you have an offer, but need to satisfy further requirements. For example, you might have just

finished an Access course and be awaiting the results. The university might want you to obtain the qualification before giving you an unconditional place. If you successfully obtain your qualification you should then get a letter from UCAS and the university confirming your acceptance.

Students who have applied for several courses may have several conditional offers, but have the option of accepting only one of these. By doing so you give a commitment to one university. You also have the option of keeping another offer as an insurance offer in case you do not meet the conditions imposed by your first choice. It is important therefore, if you have listed more than one university or course on your UCAS application form, that you choose your first and insurance offers carefully. Universities which have made you an offer may invite you to a visit day so you have an opportunity to have a look at them again.

If you do not get offered a place it might be useful to contact the university to find out if you can have some feedback, although universities are not obliged to provide this. At this point you can also go through UCAS Extra and seek a place in another university. Many students who do not get an offer, or who do not get their expected grades, enter clearing which usually happens from August and involves trawling around universities which still have places available on their courses. This process is more appropriate for students who are not restricted geographically and mature students are best advised to contact universities earlier than clearing.

Part-time study

Many mature students choose part-time study and options for flexible study are increasing. If you want to study for a degree, but work and family commitments prevent full-time study, then part-time may be the option for you. Part-time options were discussed in more detail in Chapters 5 and 6.

Applications for part-time degree study are generally made direct to the university on one of their application forms. The form will ask for personal details, information about your qualifications and employment history and there is usually a personal statement similar to that on the UCAS application form. This is where you put supporting information such as why you have chosen to return to education, why you are interested in the course and what you hope to do when you finish the course.

Other conditions of the application process

Some degree courses ask applicants to support their application in other ways in addition to the UCAS form. You may be asked to attend a one to one interview or a group interview, do an audition or present a portfolio of work. Not all applicants who submit UCAS forms get this far, so rather than seeing this as a daunting process think of it as positive feedback on your application form.

Interviews

Many degree courses relating to subjects involving interpersonal skills such as nursing, occupational therapy or counselling studies, usually ask applicants for interview as this is a valuable way of watching your interpersonal skills in action. You should be notified of the structure of the interview day in advance and it may involve a one to one or group interview. Take note of the following to ensure your interview goes well:

- Turn up on time.
- Make sure you know where you are going.
- Wear suitable smart clothing.
- Familiarize yourself with the course and the subject.
- Look at the university prospectus.
- Read what you put on your application form just in case you are asked questions about it.
- Emphasize your strengths.
- Prepare some questions to ask at the end of the interview.
- Be yourself and act naturally.

Auditions

Applicants for performance related degree courses such as dance, drama and music, will usually be invited to audition so they can demonstrate their abilities in their chosen performance area.

Portfolios

Applicants interested in art, design and creative degrees are usually asked to an interview and required to show a portfolio of their work.

Tests

Applicants for teacher training degrees often have to do an English and maths test as well as an interview. Make sure you are aware of any special requirements relating to the degree course or courses you have applied for. If you know in advance that there might be an interview or a test you will not have an unpleasant surprise if you are invited to attend one.

Checks

Some courses, such as those related to healthcare or teaching, ask applicants to undertake a medical examination and/or Criminal Records Bureau (CRB) check before you start. Find out in advance whether this applies to the course you have chosen. These are important requirements for any course which requires physical stamina, such as occupational therapy, and any course which involves contact with children and young people, such as teaching.

What next?

This chapter has introduced you to a range of qualifications, which help you prepare for higher education study and ensure you get the most out of your degree course. You should also now have an understanding of the way in which you apply for your degree course and how you can make your application stand out from the others.

The next chapter will describe what you need to do in the run up to the start of your first term.

● 9

GETTING READY FOR THE START OF TERM

This chapter will help you:

- continue your planning right up to the start of term;
- think about any other preparation you need to do before the start of term;
- survive the first week of term.

Introduction

You probably feel as though you have come a long way since you first thought about doing a degree course. Planning, preparation, study skills and completing the application form may seem a long time ago. It can be all too easy to sit back and wait for the start of the first term.

However, your planning and preparation is not over and should continue over the months or weeks leading up to the start of term. If you applied early on in the application cycle you will have quite a few months left. If your application was submitted later on you may only have a few weeks in which to prepare. Try not to panic at this stage as you should be looking forward to the degree course and congratulating yourself on getting a place. Many students do feel anxious though as the reality of their intentions comes closer.

Planning and preparation should ensure you have a realistic idea and expectation of degree level study and you should be aware what is expected of you as a student. Hopefully, there will not be any surprises, but it is best not to be complacent and essential to go through a final checklist to ensure that everything you need is in place.

Getting ready

Start date of term

Make sure you know the start date of term. Your university should contact you with details of the first day you are due to attend and the programme of activities designed to integrate you into university life.

Work commitments

If you are reducing your hours at work or giving up work altogether, make sure you give the notice required to enable you to attend university at timetabled hours. Reducing your hours, or giving up work, may be the biggest step to take, but remember you have planned and prepared for this.

If your work is related to the course you are going to do, and your employers have previously agreed to support you, ensure that your employers are still committed to you undertaking the course. Make sure you both agree on the level of support they are going to provide and preferably obtain this agreement in writing. This is particularly important if you are going to do a foundation degree with an emphasis on work-related learning. Consider the following:

- Will you need a workplace supervisor and, if so, who will it be?
- Will your employer provide you with time off for your course?
- Will your employer provide any financial help with your course costs?

Financial support for tuition fees and student loan application

If you applied for your course early on your finances should be sorted out by the start of term. If you submitted a later application you have less time in which to do this. Do a final check to make sure you have your tuition fee support and student loan in place and do not have to submit further information. If you intend to study part-time you may need to complete an application form for a fee waiver once you start your course. If your financial circumstances have changed since you applied for your tuition fee and student loans make sure you report the changes so a reassessment can be done.

Student support services

You should have found out about student support services during visits on open days, how they can help you during your time as a student and identified any special support you need to help you undertake the degree. If you have particular support requirements, and you indicated this on your UCAS application, the information may have been passed to the relevant student support service in advance of the start of term. If you have had no contact from student support services get in touch with the university and ask support staff if there is anything you need to do prior to starting. Ask if you need to speak to someone in advance about support or if there are any forms you need to complete. Chapter 10 provides more detailed information about student support services.

Enrolment/information pack

Most universities send an enrolment pack to students in the summer prior to the start of term. This may contain forms you need to return, such as financial enrolment forms, and other information about accommodation, library membership and the students' union. Find out what information you should receive before you start university.

Student guide

There should be a student guide in your enrolment pack giving information about aspects of studying, the university's policies and procedures and information about the range of support services available to students. It is unlikely you will have time to read all the information in the student guide prior to starting your course, but keep it for reference later on.

Deposit/bond

You need to find out if you are required to pay a deposit during the first week of term. Some universities ask all students to pay a deposit, regardless of whether they are staying in university accommodation or not. This is to cover any damage to university property and, should there be no damage, will be returned in full once you finish your course.

Miscellaneous costs

Make sure you have worked out all your miscellaneous costs such as transport to and from university, car parking, an amount for food and drinks each day, textbooks, special equipment, photocopying costs and stationery. Try to be realistic about these costs; it is better to overestimate than underestimate.

Council tax

Make enquiries about a discount on your Council tax. You will probably need a form from the university to confirm you are a student before you can apply for the discount and therefore may not be able to arrange your discount until the beginning of term.

Paperwork and certificates

Make sure you reply to any letters from UCAS and the university and have provided any information they ask for, such as certificates showing your qualifications. Keep your paperwork organized in a file so you can refer to it easily if you need to. If you have been given a conditional offer on the basis of obtaining a qualification make sure you inform the university and UCAS once your result comes through.

Accommodation

If you are moving into student accommodation you should receive relevant information before the start of term including what you need to take with you, such as bedding or crockery, and when you can arrive. You will also need to complete a tenancy agreement and find out what sort of payment you need to make in advance. If you have not been given this information contact the university's accommodation office. Do not forget to organize insurance of your possessions. Finally, let the accommodation office know if you have any special requirements, for example, a room on the ground floor if you have a disability.

Moving away to study

If you are moving away to study you will need to make a list of all the organizations you need to contact and inform about your change of address.

Library membership

You may have the opportunity to register with the university library by mail in advance of the first week of term. This does not necessarily mean you will be able to use the library prior to starting, but gives you less to do once you start term. The first week of term will be busy so try to do as much in advance as possible.

Photographs

Make sure you have a good supply of passport photographs before you start and get at least four. You may need these for your library registration, financial registration and your students' union card.

Reading lists

You may be sent a reading list in advance of the start of term, although this practice varies from university to university. Do not be tempted to go out and buy every book on the list; you do not need to, it will cost too much to do so and most of the books should be in the university library. If the university has indicated essential texts you may find it useful to buy these, but check first by contacting the university. If they indicate that it would be useful to do some background reading prior to starting make sure this is part of your preparation.

Special equipment

You may need to buy special equipment if you are doing a practical courses such as art or sport. You should have considered these costs some time back and therefore have a good idea of the type of equipment you need to buy. Try not to leave this to the last minute as you may then end up with a large amount of expense in one go.

Getting organized

Make sure you are organized at home and ready for when you start your course.

- Have you got space to study at home?
- Have you got a computer and can you use it?
- Will you be able to find time to study in peace and quiet?

I wish I had organized my study space at home better. I ended up with boxes and books everywhere.

(Foundation degree in rehabilitation student)

Open day

If the university has an open day before the start of your course, try to attend. It may have been some time since you visited and if you visit again it will make you feel better about your first week and more familiar with the university. Some universities organize visit days for people who have applied and have been given an offer of a place. This provides an opportunity to ask last minute questions.

The first week

I have vivid memories of my first few days at college. I was overwhelmed by thoughts that I had fooled myself into thinking that I had the ability to study for a degree. However, the gloom soon lifted and I settled into studying.

(English literature and women's studies degree graduate)

The first week of term can prove to be difficult for students and a likely time for them to decide to leave and not return. The first week usually has an organized timetable of information and academic sessions and social activities. At the end of the week you will have taken in so much information you may be wondering why you decided to return to studying. Certainly by the end of the week you may have been allocated an academic tutor, registered for your introductory modules, received your membership card for the library, been allocated access to IT facilities, had a campus tour, met some of your fellow students and had the opportunity of attending a number of social events. You should also have a timetable for your course and many students find they settle in once they get into the routine of lectures and seminars.

There will probably be a 'freshers' fair' in the first few weeks of term. This is an opportunity to find out information about the university social and sporting activities. The temptation is to sign up for everything of interest, but you probably won't have enough time to commit to this. Be careful about what you sign up for.

Do not expect the first week or weeks to be easy, but treat it just as you would a new job. It takes time to get to know people, to get used to the new environment and the way things are done.

What next?

You should now be prepared and have everything in place for the start of term. This isn't to say that the unexpected will not happen or that you will have remembered all the things you need to do, but you will have sorted out the most important elements of your planning and preparation.

The next chapter provides advice about the support you can expect to get as a student, what to do if it starts to go wrong and suggestions for how to keep motivated.

10

KEEPING GOING TO THE END

This chapter will help you:

- understand what sort of support you can get when you are a student;
- understand what to do if you feel it's all going wrong;
- explore ways in which you can keep motivated to study;
- examine what coping strategies you can use to help you keep going.

With the vast amount of support I have received from family, friends and fellow students I now know the decision I took in returning to higher education was the right one and I can only give it my best shot.

(Design and technology degree student)

Introduction

You've started your first term at university and now the really hard work begins. This chapter looks at ways in which you can get support and help while you study and emphasizes the importance of asking for help if and when you need to. There are suggestions about how you can maintain your motivation and ways in which you can cope with the unexpected.

Student support services

Higher education students, of any age, are not expected to exist in isolation and there are a range of student support services in universities whose purpose is to help you. Ask for help when you need it and do not feel ashamed or embarrassed to do this. You may find you get through your degree course without having to access any student support, however most students will, at some point, need to seek advice. Generally the student support services offered in any university are as follows.

Disability support

This service helps students who have a physical or mental disability by providing support and advice. Examples of the types of support offered include arranging for someone to accompany you to lectures and take notes if you have a hearing impairment, providing alternative arrangements for examinations if you have dyslexia, providing a learning mentor, or advising about the range of financial support available. Chapter 6 outlined some of the financial support available for students with disabilities and if you are unsure about your entitlement always seek further guidance from the university.

Case study

Simon had particular support requirements and investigated the support services offered in a number of universities. The pre-admissions support, study skills support and disability support offered in one of them was, he felt, far better than in others. He made his decision to study there on the basis of how he was supported before he attended the university. In his opinion this reflected on the support he would get during his time as a student there.

Mature student support

Some universities have a specific mature student adviser and might organize meetings and social gatherings for mature students. If your university does not do this you might consider starting a mature student group if you think there is a need for one.

Writing support

Writing support services offer support to any student finding difficulty with study skills such as essay writing or time management. They may also offer a diagnostic service for dyslexic students followed by on-going support. Your access to writing support may be limited to one or two sessions, but check this out with the service in advance. They may also be able to provide you with handouts on study skills or these may be accessible on the university website.

Student finance advisers

You might get to know these staff very well during your time in university. Find out as soon as possible who they are and where they are located so you can access this service whenever you need to. Managing on a student budget is a challenge and finance advisers usually provide advice on budgeting and administer special funds to award to students in financial difficulty. This can make the difference between staying on your course or having to leave so do not be too proud to ask for help. All universities have special funds and usually students have to apply in writing for this help, giving information about their income, benefit receipt, bank statements and any special circumstances affecting them. You may, for instance, have extra childcare costs because of your lecture timetable, or extra household costs because you have an adult dependent who is ill. Never be afraid to ask for help.

Case study

Rebecca had a parent who was ill and receiving treatment on a regular basis. The student was studying some way from home and was making more return trips home to be with their parent and support their family. She was able to claim some of the travel costs out of the university's special funds, because of the particular circumstances of her parent's illness. This helped tremendously at a difficult time.

Childcare facilities

This provision will vary from university to university. Some run their own subsidized childcare facilities while others may franchise the service to privately run organizations. This is something you need to check out when you visit universities on open days. Find out the situation in your university. Even if you have no need at present for the childcare offered and have organized your own, you may find you need to access the university's childcare later on. Most nurseries will give you a tour of their facilities if you ask for one and answer any questions you have.

Students' union

Most universities have a students' union affiliated to the National Union of Students. The students' union has elected officers (usually current students or recent graduates) and represents the students' voice in a number of ways. Elected officers are often members of various university committees and can ensure students' opinions are known and heard.

The students' union also coordinates a range of clubs and societies, covering activities from sports to music to mountaineering. There should be something for everyone. They may organize a mature students' group and although time may be limited it is worth joining as this will help you meet other mature students.

As a member of the students' union, and therefore the National Union of Students, you qualify for a range of discounts in a variety of shops, clubs and bars. You may also be entitled to a student railcard. Find out early on what discounts you can get and make full use of them.

Welfare advice

This service may be offered by the university or by the students' union. Either way the welfare adviser will be able to advise about benefits, finance, legal issues, consumer rights, housing, debt and a whole range of other issues. Welfare advisers should preferably be qualified advisers with experience and expertise in support work.

Counselling and guidance

This service provides pastoral care to students in a non-judgemental, confidential way. Do not be afraid to access counselling support if any anxieties start to become too big to cope with on your own.

Academic tutors

You should be allocated an academic tutor early on in your first term. Your tutor should be a member of academic staff who will help you with any academic support you need. For example, you may not be sure about your progress or feel lacking in confidence in your academic ability. Your tutor should be able to provide feedback to you and advice about assignments. If they feel you are not making progress, they should provide constructive comments about how you can improve. It is in their interests to make sure you are progressing well in your studies. Try to maintain a balance in your contact with them; if you try to see them every day they will soon tire of helping you.

Careers service

There are a variety of ways in which the careers service in your university can help you. They might provide workshops on topics such as job hunting, how to complete an application form and interview skills, or advise you how to make the most of a work placement. If you are unsure which career you would like to follow the careers service will be able to provide a one to one interview with a qualified careers adviser and has a range of resources you can access to help you make a decision. Many services keep records of local part-time work suitable for students.

Spiritual support

For many students this is an important part of the university environment and there should be provision for students of all faiths with pastoral as well as spiritual support.

Health centre

All students should have the opportunity to register with the university health centre. If you are a mature student and are studying locally, you will probably already be registered with a health centre. However, if there is a health centre on the university campus check out what services they provide and what services you can access should you wish to.

It's all going wrong

Despite careful thought and planning sometimes students get the feeling that all is not well and is not going to get better.

The wrong course

It might become apparent early on that you have chosen a course that doesn't suit you, and it's best if you *do* realize this early on, rather than in the third year of the course. Students can try to change course if they have chosen the wrong one, but this should be done in the first term or year. Universities may allow you to change, but it depends what course you want to change to and whether there are places on it, so do not take it for granted that you can. If you feel you have chosen the wrong course speak to your academic tutor as soon as possible. Try to make sure you are not just feeling out of place and this is affecting your feelings about the course. Also check your financial situation regarding tuition fees before you make your final decision.

The wrong university

You may find it difficult to settle in because you are in a new environment. Alternatively you may dislike the environment and realize you are not likely to settle in. Speak to a tutor or to a member of student services about how you feel. It is a major decision to change university and this should not be done without careful consideration. You may find there are no places left in the university you want to change to and might have to wait another year before applying again.

Too much work

However much planning you have done in advance it can be difficult to estimate the academic workload and you only really find this out once you start. If you are finding it hard to cope, and realize early on that you have taken on too much, discuss this with your academic tutor or with a member of student services staff. If you are studying full-time you might be advised to change to part-time study if the course you are doing is available to study on a part-time basis. It will take you longer to complete your course, but at least you will still be studying.

Financial problems

Many students will encounter financial problems. If yours are beginning to get out of hand, and you have debts which are attracting an unhealthy interest from credit companies, get some advice straight away. Go to your student finance advisers and local Citizens' Advice Bureau rather than pretending the problem does not exist.

Withdrawing from your course

Some students find they have to withdraw from their degree course because of mitigating circumstances, which make continuing impossible. This could be because of illness, family problems, finance, divorce or bereavement. Do not just leave your course without speaking to someone at the university. Get some advice, check the amount of credits you have already accumulated on the course and find out if you would be able to come back and study at a future date once you have resolved your problems. If you have enjoyed studying, but have to leave and will miss the routine of it, consider doing a short adult education course in the meantime. This will keep you studying and provide you with an interest and a focus while you sort things out. It should also help you feel less anxious about returning to your degree course in the future.

Keeping motivated

However motivated you are at the beginning of your course, there will be times when you feel as though you do not want to carry on studying or you feel fed up with essay deadlines and lectures. This is natural and you will not be the only student who feels this way. Most students find it difficult to maintain their motivation throughout the duration of their degree. Be prepared for this and be ready to take steps to raise your motivation levels whenever you need to.

Remind yourself why you are doing the degree course. Keep doing this and reflect on what you were doing before. If you are doing the course because you wanted to escape from a dead end job, think about a day in that job and how you felt. If you have been made redundant think about what else you might be doing if you had decided not to do the degree. Do not lose sight of your reasons for doing the course and refer back to Chapter 1 whenever you forget what motivated you in the first place.

> Prior to starting university I thought I was stupid, beyond learning and starting over. I really didn't believe I was good enough to go on to higher education, yet now I'm full of confidence. I believe I can achieve anything I set my mind to, and it's up to me to prove it!

> Returning to learning has changed me for the better. I'm a better mum as I'm happier. I can lead by example and take pride in myself and my achievements. I really like who I've grown into and believe that the whole experience has prepared me well for the future. I could never turn back or have any regrets.
>
> (Drama degree student)

Remember you had to apply for your course and were given an offer of a place. Look upon this as a show of confidence in your ability to study. It is not in the university's interest to offer a place to students who they think will not be able to cope with studying at degree level.

Recognize achievements while you study, however small you think they may be. Meeting a deadline for an essay is an achievement, so is attending a long (and possibly boring) lecture or managing to read a difficult chapter in an academic text book. Measure achievements in small steps and as you realize what you are achieving your motivation will increase.

Congratulate yourself on assignments for which you get good marks. If you get a B do not waste time wishing you had got an A. If you do this you will never be happy with your marks. Think positively if you have not got as good an assessment as you thought you might get. Regard critical feedback as constructive criticism and look at and take notice of the pointers given in your feedback from the tutor so you can improve your work in the future.

You may not enjoy every module on the degree course. It is only natural that you will enjoy some more than others, but you have to persevere with the ones you do not enjoy if they are compulsory. Remember, every module is like a short course in itself and there is an end in sight and hopefully a more enjoyable module available in the future.

> I think most mature students have more drive, desire and reason to be doing what they are doing; and more discipline and will to succeed.
>
> (History degree graduate)

Coping strategies

You may have planned and prepared for the course and considered every aspect of the decision you made. However, you cannot plan life in every detail and the unexpected will always happen. Try to put your own support systems in place to cover every eventuality.

This may involve asking favours from family and friends and do not be afraid to do so. If you involved them in your decision making all along they will already be aware of why you are doing what you are doing. There is every possibility that you can return favours later on and you can let your friends and family know that you intend to do so.

Work with your fellow students and provide support to each other when you need it. Always ask for help if you need it.

What next?

The chapter has outlined the various support services available to students, provided guidance about what to do if you feel it's all going wrong and given advice about how to keep motivated.

It helps to end on a positive note. Many mature students gain tremendously from their degree studies and manage to get to the end of their course and gain a qualification and a job they enjoy. I hope you will be one of these students. Good luck with your studies.

> Go for it – it will be one of the most rewarding experiences of your life.
>
> (English literature degree graduate)

11

CAREER PROSPECTS
Leila Roberts

Introduction

It is worth thinking about your future, even early in your studies, as the choices you make could affect your eventual job chances.

A degree is a big commitment, not least in time and money, and many people undertake one in the hope that it will lead to a better job. In general, this is justified: being a graduate has, historically, meant that you are likely to earn more, have less chance of unemployment and will gain more promotions; as well as the less tangible personal benefits a degree can bring. However, a degree is not an automatic passport to employment and prosperity – you will need other 'career skills' to be able to make the most of your opportunities. This chapter will look at graduate prospects, and what you can do to increase your chances of getting a job you enjoy.

What is a graduate job?

Many people have outdated ideas about what graduates do and what they earn. Graduates are still thought of as a privileged, high-earning elite who don't have 'jobs' but have 'careers' (often implying a progression in one occupation). There is some truth in this, but it can also be unhelpful. Let's look at why.

Mature students, more than most, will realize that work is changing all the time. New technologies mean that some jobs disappear and new ones are created. The globalization of world markets has also hugely affected the types of work we do (manufacturing is increasingly moving to cheaper countries) and management fads change how we structure work ('downsizing' and 'de-layering', cut workforces and flattened hierarchies). Change is constant. Few people do the same job in the same way for any length of time. The idea of choosing a 'career for life' seems increasingly outdated.

At the same time, the number of students entering higher education has grown enormously – from 6 per cent in 1960 to nearer 43 per cent today. Graduates are no longer a small elite. They also study a much greater variety of subjects – equine studies, dance, sports science – none of these were offered thirty years ago.

All this has affected graduate jobs. Graduates now do a much wider range of jobs with a much more varied range of employers than they did in the past. Some jobs which used to be non-graduate now routinely ask for graduates, but the jobs will probably have changed. At the same time, many graduates go into work where a degree is not a specific requirement. Although there are still designated graduate training schemes in large organizations, very many graduates will find employment with smaller, more diverse organizations – or will be self-employed.

Is the degree vocational?

It's also important to note that while, of course, many graduates go into jobs related to their degree studies, many don't. You are not a failure if you go into a job which has no obvious connection with your degree subject – in fact this is entirely normal. Many graduate jobs ask for a degree in 'any subject': employers will be looking for other skills and intellectual qualities which you have developed as part of your degree, not necessarily the 'knowledge content' of your studies.

However, if you are intending to study a course *specifically* because you think it is vocational, do check it out. Don't just assume that if it *sounds* vocational, there are hosts of employers waiting to offer you jobs. Ask the course tutors, and also contact the University's careers service, which may be able to provide impartial information on what sort of jobs previous graduates have gone into. Check out the Prospects website (www.Prospects.ac.uk) for graduate destinations; if possible, talk to past graduates. Some courses have an impressive record of graduates moving into related jobs; others may be interesting courses to study but, in fact, are not necessarily preparing you for work in this area.

Graduate prospects

Over a lifetime, the figures show that graduates can expect to earn more than non-graduates (especially graduate women compared with non-graduate women, although they still lag behind graduate men). However, these figures are looking at the careers of people who entered the workforce when graduates were a small minority. We simply don't know how, when graduates approach 50 per cent of a cohort, they will fare in terms of prospects and prosperity. The press annually prints reports of graduate earnings which often are based only on those working for prestigious companies. In fact graduate salaries vary as much as graduate jobs; a recent survey showed a range of £5,000 p.a. to £40,000 starting salaries, with most clustering between £10,000 and £20,000 for new graduates.

For mature students this is bad news and good. The bad news is that getting a better job won't be automatic – it will require a lot of effort. The good news is that there are now much wider opportunities for graduates. Also, in general, being a graduate will give you the chance to have a more fulfilling career. But you need the skills to make the most of that opportunity.

Improving your career prospects

It's easy for students to become fixated on course marks, as if good marks alone will make you employable. In practice, if you can build up your 'career management skills' you can dramatically increase your chances of finding enjoyable work. These skills include:

- being able to identify work you would enjoy;
- finding opportunities;
- being able to present yourself effectively on paper and in person.

It is impossible in a short chapter to explain these in detail, so I will give an overview, covering issues of particular relevance to mature students, and will guide you to further reading.

Identifying work you might enjoy

One of the main reasons for doing a degree is to 'get a better job', by which students usually mean a personally rewarding and fulfilling one. However, 'fulfilment' means different things to different people: it could mean, for example, more money, or status, or challenge, or a chance to contribute to something worthwhile. There are different theories about how people find congenial work, but in practice most will concentrate on helping you identify

- your personal key values – that is, what you personally want from work;
- the skills you enjoy using – (many people find it difficult to articulate the skills they have, but employers will ask for evidence of your skills);
- your interests – the people and things you enjoy spending time on or working with.

The good news is that there are tried and tested methods of identifying your values, skills, interests and other elements in career choice. All university and college careers services will have information on them and many institutions will run careers education courses to help undergraduates. (Recommended books and websites are given below.)

Collecting evidence

It is worth thinking about your CV throughout your course, especially if you have a specific career in mind. By thinking about your CV you will be actively *collecting evidence* of your suitability for employment: by choosing relevant modules, by taking advantage of any extra-curricular activities which may be useful to you and, most of all, by taking advantage of any work placement opportunities. If you're given the opportunity to compile a 'graduate profile', (a record and reflection upon your student life) this could be invaluable as a way of focusing upon what you are learning and how it might be relevant to your future options.

Making the most of a work placement

Many mature students complain bitterly about having to do a work placement, seeing it purely in terms of 'work experience'. Quite reasonably, they argue, if you have already had years of experience why do you need a placement? In fact a placement can be *especially* useful for mature students. It can build confidence, be a bridge from your previous employment into a better or more congenial job, give you the opportunity to use your new skills in a practical situation and, most importantly, give you the chance to make contacts which could be helpful after you graduate (see 'networking', below).

So it's worth giving careful thought to the placement, and trying to organize one where you can build on your academic learning, or are doing work you may be interested in after graduating. Getting a placement is often frustrating and time consuming, but be careful about taking an easy option; the placement is a real opportunity which you would be wise to take seriously. Every year many students get job offers as a direct result of their placement – either with the organization where they worked, or because the placement gave their CV just the required boost.

Here are some of the opportunities a placement may provide:

Academic enrichment

- Skills or techniques you have learned in the classroom may be put into practice.
- Theoretical understanding can be observed and tested in real life.

Career development

- You can investigate work you're interested in doing, identifying what skills or personal qualities are needed.
- Employment opportunities in this field can be investigated, with this or other organizations.
- You can get ideas about related occupations or other employers.
- Your university reference will be boosted.

Skills development

During your degree you will be developing many skills, but to be able to present them to employers you need to be aware of them and give evidence of where you have used them. These skills might include:

- mathematical: numeracy, statistics, graphs, measuring, interpreting, etc.;
- communication: written (reports, letters, memos, texts); oral (listening; presentations, meetings, interviews, etc.);
- IT;
- interpersonal: negotiating, teamworking, decision making;
- time management: organizing your workload, having a sense of urgency, prioritising, delegating, etc.;
- those specific to your degree subject.

Confidence building

Finding that you can be useful, can 'fit in' to a team, that your skills have worth and can be used to make things happen, can be a tremendous confidence boost.

Investigating employers

Placements can be with all sizes of organization, from large corporations to one-man bands, but it is always helpful to develop an awareness of what the organization is about. This will help you in choosing a type of organization you would enjoy working for (including working for yourself), and in putting together a good application. (Employers often complain that graduates show little awareness of the business focus of the organization they're applying to.)

Researching opportunities

All graduates develop research skills, but few think to use those skills in their job hunting. However, researching opportunities is a key career skill. Every year graduates get jobs with organizations which have not necessarily advertised vacancies: this 'creative job hunting' technique can be especially valuable for mature students. It can help you identify unusual jobs, or be useful if you are restricted to a particular geographical area. For example, some mature graduates will need to look for employment near their home: in this case it's useful to think not in terms of 'I need to work in York', for example, but how much time you are willing to give to travelling to work. If you research travelling times and public transport options then you should get a radius of places where you might feasibly look for work.

What is creative job hunting? It involves detailed research in a job area, including conducting 'information interviews' with people who are doing the job you're interested in. This research can really help you in many ways. You can use it to:

- make an informed decision about whether you would want to do this work;
- target your CV or application form to the precise requirements of the job;
- make contacts – even, if you are lucky, make an impression.

Every year students are offered vacation work, placements or jobs on the strength of information interviews. Information interviews are a great opportunity to start 'networking'.

'Networking'

Recruitment is expensive – and interviews are notoriously ineffective as a way of predicting if someone will be good at a job. The ideal way for an organization to fill a vacancy is to employ someone they know. This is why many people get job offers as a result of placements, voluntary work or temporary work, or simply through contacts. As a student, you have perfect 'cover' for investigating different occupations and 'networking'. Do use all your resources: family, friends, colleagues in part-time work, tutors, the alumni association, the careers service; all can help you in making contacts.

Presenting yourself: forms and CVs

When you're asked to complete an application form, or compile a CV for a specific job, the employer will always be looking for how your skills, experience and personal qualities match the specifications of the job. A CV, in particular, should address the job requirements, not be simply a list of things you have done. It follows that the more *evidence* you can give for having these skills, qualities, etc., the higher your chances of getting the job.

Forms and CVs should therefore be crafted carefully to focus on the job description and what the employer is looking for. They are your evidence of your suitability.

Here are a few tips:

- Value your life experiences. Look for evidence in all areas of your life as well as your studies, e.g. home, hobbies, voluntary work. If you have children, for example, you probably have developed excellent skills in organization and time management. You may have developed teamworking skills through voluntary work or the PTA. Skills are skills no matter where you developed them.
- Think creatively about your studies. A literature student applying for social work might not have any directly relevant modules but may have covered things like multicultural issues, which could be useful.
- Don't leave out information: if it isn't written down, the employer won't know about it.
- If you have had many short-term jobs you may need to summarize them, emphasizing the most relevant. Try to show any progression (e.g. in responsibility) or repeat employment with the same employer (which shows you were valued).
- Don't forget any training you have had in earlier employment, e.g. short courses.
- Voluntary work could be as useful as paid work in demonstrating what you can do.
- Investigate different types of CV not just simple chronological lists: these may help you 'sell yourself' more effectively. Keep CVs to two pages maximum.
- If you have unusual qualifications explain what they are and how you got them: night school, for example, may show perseverance and high motivation.
- If you are an older graduate you may need to explain, in your covering letter, what led to your career change and what your career plans are.

Interviews

Employers use an interview to test the evidence you gave in your application form or CV. They are already thinking that you are potentially the right candidate – your job now is to convince them. They will want to find out:

- can you do the job? (i.e. do you have the right experience or qualifications?)
Have a strong sense of what you have to offer, and what evidence
you are going to present. Make sure you get across the areas where
your experience strongly matches the job description, and be prepared to answer questions on those areas where your experience is
weakest.
- will you do the job? (i.e. how well motivated are you?)
Research the job and the organization – you will come across as
highly motivated and keen.
- will you fit in?
Be polite and friendly with everyone you meet, from the moment
you walk in to the moment you leave. (Remember too that interviews give you the chance to decide if you would like to work here.)

Tips:

- Be positive, polite and well-prepared. Have a strong sense of what
you have to offer, and what evidence you are going to present.
- Never diminish your achievements through using 'just' or 'only'.
Don't say 'I was only a housewife ...', rather, 'I was a mother
managing a household and two small children'.
- You may be faced with a young and inexperienced interviewer. Be
friendly and professional.
- Show enthusiasm for the job.
- If faced with age discrimination stay calm and positive about all the
'life skills' which come with maturity. Your degree studies show that
you are flexible, adaptable and can learn quickly.

Age discrimination

It does exist, and it's worth thinking through your strategies if con-
fronted by it: be prepared to emphasize what you have to offer.

Employers' worries about employing older people often focus on
things like higher pay expectations, retention, mobility restrictions,
and having older people 'fit in' with younger colleagues. You can
tackle these by pointing out that few employees these days stay with
organizations for a long time and there is evidence that mature employees actually stay longer and are more reliable in terms of sick leave
etc. than younger ones. Emphasize your maturity, high motivation

and life-honed social skills. If you have studied for a degree it does suggest that you can happily mix with younger people!

Being confident

One issue that older graduates always raise is confidence. Confidence has been described as an essential attribute for success: if you are the ablest person in the world, but haven't got the confidence to use your talents, they're not much use to you. However, many people lack confidence, especially when making transitions from one job to another or from study to work. Often people think everyone else is confident, except themselves!

Here are a few tips on building confidence.

Think positively

Most of us have an inner critical voice in our head, commenting on our inadequacies. Many women, in particular, say that they often feel 'a fraud' and are afraid of being 'found out' even when they're functioning perfectly well. This 'bad angel' voice is demoralizing and useless.

Step 1 in building confidence is to give the bad angel the boot. Allow yourself a 'good angel', and let this positive encouraging voice be heard: 'That was difficult but you got through it!' 'You handled that well.' 'You can do this!' 'Have a go!'

If you go into an interview thinking 'I've got no chance', you probably won't have, because your negative attitude will come over in your voice, body language and statements. But just as mental attitude works in a negative way it also works the other way round: positive thinking works too! So boost yourself with 'I can do this'; 'I am confident and happy'. (Always make statements in the present tense: 'I am successful'). Try it and see what happens.

Be aware of your strengths

When we do something well, we often assume it's something everyone can do. (But when we find something difficult we assume everyone else finds it easy.) Acknowledge the things you do well and feel good about them, because competence gives you confidence.

Competence is being able to perform something reliably to an acceptable standard. It's not the same as being perfect and never making mistakes.

To be competent you have to:

- have most of the required skills and knowledge;
- have a good attitude: be willing, constructive, positive;
- pay attention to what you are doing, how you are performing and how you could do better next time. Learn from your mistakes.

Think about all the skills you developed as a student, and those you gained in your working life. List them. Keep looking at this list – it will boost your spirits.

Set yourself goals

If you divide your goals into small steps, and systematically achieve them, you are building confidence. (Conversely, if you fall into a habit of setting yourself goals and letting them slide, this can really demoralize you). If you break a major goal into small achievable parts, and keep fulfilling them, you will be riding on a tide of success. Success really does build success. Making small steps can lead to the accomplishment of major goals.

Have a go

We develop confidence by doing. Even if it doesn't work out – you tried!

Look and act the part

Have a positive mental image of who you want to be and act as if you were that person. How you regard yourself affects the way other people treat you. Don't be afraid to adopt the appropriate 'role' for the situation: we all have to use different roles in different aspects of our lives.

Degree studies can be challenging – even daunting. But overcoming challenges is how we build confidence. Most students feel that during their studies they have learned a lot, widened their mental outlook, built confidence through a track record of success, and 'grown' both professionally and personally.

Summary

- Graduates work in a very wide range of jobs with all sizes of employer including self-employment. Salaries vary widely.
- A degree can increase your chances of a fulfilling job, but you need 'career skills' too.
- Be aware that you are building your CV throughout your studies.
- Make the most of a work placement.
- Research opportunities and 'network'.

Further information

There are many books on **career choice and job hunting**, such as:

Roberts, L. (2006) *After You Graduate*. Maidenhead: Open University Press.
Bolles, R. N. (2006) *What Color Is Your Parachute?* Ten Speed Press.

There are also many useful websites including the one run by University Careers Services at www.Prospects.ac.uk
A recommended book on **confidence** is:
Jeffers, S. (1997) *Feel The Fear and Do It Anyway*. London: Rider.

Your careers service

All universities and colleges of HE will have a careers service. In most, you will have the opportunity to browse the careers library and to see a careers advisor (although some are very busy in term time). The careers library will have information on all sorts of different occupations, national and local employers, overseas opportunities, postgraduate courses, voluntary work, etc. It will also have tips on making applications and improving your interview techniques, including videos. Do make the most of this resource. You may be surprised at the range of information a good careers library holds.

HOW TO GET FURTHER ADVICE

Careers

Careers Wales
www.careerswales.com
Provides information and advice on learning and career opportunities in Wales.

Connexions
Tel: 080 800 13219
www.connexions.gov.uk
Offers information and guidance for people aged from 13 to 19 years old and young people up to the age of 25 with disabilities.

Guidance Enterprises Group
www.guidance-enterprises.co.uk
Provider of career and personal development products. Gives advice to adults and young people about careers and training opportunities.

Learndirect
Tel: 0800 100 900
www.learndirect.co.uk
Information and advice on learning and work opportunities.

National Health Service Careers
Tel: 0845 60 60 655
www.nhscareers.nhs.uk
Information and advice about careers in the National Health Service.

Open University Careers Advisory Service
www.open.ac.uk/careers

Training and Development Agency for Schools
PO Box 3210
Chelmsford
Essex CM1 3WA
Tel: 0845 6000 991 (English speakers), 0845 6000 992 (Welsh speakers)
www.tda.gov.uk
Information and advice about training for primary and secondary school teaching.

Worktrain
www.worktrain.gov.uk
Information about jobs, training and job vacancies.

Careers for graduates

Graduate Prospects
www.prospects.ac.uk
Provides a graduate careers support service and is a subsidiary of the Higher Education Careers Services Unit.

Return to learn courses

Learndirect
Tel: 0800 100 900
www.learndirect.co.uk
Information and advice on learning and work opportunities and on computer courses.

National Institute of Adult Continuing Education (NIACE)
Renaissance House
20 Princess Road West
Leicester
LE1 6TP
Tel: 0116 204 4200
www.niace.org.uk
An organization which promotes adult education.

Workers Educational Association (WEA)
Temple House
17 Victoria Park Square
London E2 9PB
Tel: 020 8983 1515
www.wea.org.uk
Offers a wide range of adult education courses throughout the UK.

Course and university choice

Aimhigher
www.aimhigher.ac.uk
Aimhigher produces a variety of literature and information relating to higher education. Although primarily aimed at school leavers, much of it is relevant to and useful for mature students.

Foundation degrees
www.foundationdegree.org.uk
For information on foundation degrees.

Higher Education Funding Council (HEFCE)
Northavon House
Coldharbour Lane
Bristol BS16 1QD
Tel: 0117 931 7317
www.hefce.ac.uk
HEFCE provides information on institutional performance indicators to aid course and university choice.

Higher Education Funding Council for Wales (HEFCW)
Tel: 029 2076 1861
www.elwa.org.uk
HEFCW provides information on institutional performance indicators to aid course and university choice.

Higher Education Statistics Agency (HESA)
www.hesa.ac.uk
HESA produces reviews relating to individual institutions to aid course and university choice.

Quality Assurance Agency for Higher Education (QAA)
Southgate House
Southgate Street
Gloucester GL1 1UB
Tel: 01452 557000
www.qaa.ac.uk

Scottish Higher Education Funding Council (SHEFC)
www.shefc.ac.uk
SHEFC provides information on institutional performance indicators to aid course and university choice.

Teaching Quality Information (TQI)
www.tqi.ac.uk
Website providing information relating to individual institutions, such as completion rates and achievement rates.

Universities and Colleges Admissions Service (UCAS)
Rosehill
New Barn Lane
Cheltenham
Glos GL52 3ZD
Tel: 01242 222444
www.ucas.ac.uk
UCAS coordinates admissions to full-time degree courses. They have a comprehensive website, and print based guides, listing courses in the UK. They are also the point of contact for the UCAS application form for full-time courses.

Distance learning

Open University
PO Box 724
Milton Keynes
MK7 6ZS
Tel: 0870 333 4340
www.open.ac.uk
The largest provider of distance learning in the UK with 150,000 learners.

Finance

The system in use will vary depending on whether you choose to study in England, Wales, Scotland or Northern Ireland. Contact the following, or visit their websites, for up to date information on financial support.

England

Department for Education and Skills helpline
Tel: 01325 392822

Department for Education and Skills publications
Tel: 0800 731 9133
www.dfes.gov.uk/studentsupport

NHS Bursaries in England
NHS Student Grants Unit
Hesketh House
200–220 Broadway
Fleetwood
Lancashire FY7 8SS
Tel: 0845 358 6655
www.nhspa.gov.uk

Northern Ireland

Student Finance Branch
Department for Employment and Learning
Adelaide House
39–49 Adelaide Street
Belfast
BT2 8FD
Tel: 028 9025 7777
www.delni.gov.uk

Scotland

Student Awards Agency for Scotland
Gyleview House
3 Redheughs Rigg
South Gyle
Edinburgh EH12 9HH
Tel: 0845 111 1711
www.saas.gov.uk
(Also contact them for details about NHS bursaries in Scotland.)

Wales

Welsh Assembly Government
HED2
3rd Floor
Cathays Park
Cardiff CF10 3NQ
Tel: 029 2082 5831
www.learning.wales.gov.uk

NHS Bursaries in Wales
NHS Wales Student Awards Unit
2nd Floor
Golate House
101 St Mary's Street
Cardiff CF10 1DX
Tel: 029 2026 1495
www.hpw.org.uk

General contacts

Benefits Enquiry Line
Tel (England, Scotland, Wales): 0800 88 22 00
Tel (Northern Ireland): 0800 220 674
www.dss.gov.uk

Career Development Loans
Tel: 0800 585 505
www.lifelonglearning.co.uk/cdl

Citizens' Advice Bureau
www.citizensadvice.org.uk

Consumer Credit Counselling Service
Tel: 0800 138 1111
www.cccs.co.uk

Educational Grants Advisory Service (information about sources of funding)
501–505 Kingsland Road
London E8 4AU
Tel: 020 7254 6251
www.egas-online.org.uk

Funderfinder
www.funderfinder.org.uk
Develops and distributes software to help people identify charities and trusts for funding.

General Social Care Council (for social work bursaries)
Bursaries Office
Goldings House
2 Hay's Lane
London SE1 2HB
Tel: 020 7397 5835

National Consumer Council
Tel: 020 7730 3469
www.ncc.org.uk

National Debtline
Tel: 0808 808 4000
www.nationaldebtline.co.uk

Skill (information for students with disabilities)
Chapter House
18–20 Crucifix Lane
London SE1 3JW
Information line: 0800 328 5050
www.skill.org.uk

Student Loans Company Limited
100 Bothwell Street
Glasgow
G2 7JD
Tel: 0800 40 50 10
Minicom: 0800 085 3950
www.slc.co.uk

Student support

Childcare Link
Tel: 0800 096 0296
www.childcarelink.gov.uk
Information on local services and factsheets on childcare options.

National Union of Students (NUS)
461 Holloway Road
London
N7 6LZ
Tel: 020 7272 8900
www.nusonline.co.uk

Nightline
www.nightline.niss.ac.uk
A welfare service and telephone helpline for students, run by students.

RECOMMENDED READING

Careers

Bolles, R.N. (2005) *What Color is your Parachute?* California: Ten Speed Press.
Hopson, B., Scally, M. (1999) *Build Your Own Rainbow. A Workbook for Career and Life Management.* Chalford: Management Books.
Roberts, L. (2006). After you graduate. Maidenhead: Open University Press.

Computer skills

Miller, M. (2002) *Absolute Beginner's Guide to Computers and the Internet.* Indianapolis, IN: Que Publishers.
Most large bookshops will have a wide range of computing books.

Distance learning

Talbot, C. (2003) *Studying at a Distance: A Guide for Students.* Maidenhead: Open University Press.

Study skills

Bell, J. (2005) *Doing your Research Project.* Buckingham: Open University Press.
Buzan, T. (2003) *The Mind Map Book,* 3rd edn. London: BBC Books.
Cottrell, S. (2003) *The Study Skills Handbook,* 2nd edn. Basingstoke: Palgrave Macmillan.

Creme, P., Lea, M.R. (1997) *Writing at University: A Guide for Students*. Maidenhead: Open University Press.

De Bono, E. (1970) *Lateral Thinking*. London: Penguin Books.

Gardener, H. (1993) *Frames of Mind: The Theory of Multiple Intelligences*, 2nd edn. London: Fontana.

Honey, P., Mumford, A. (1986) *Using Your Learning Styles*. Maidenhead: Peter Honey.

King, G. (2003) *Collins Good Writing Guide: The Essential Guide to Good Writing*. Glasgow: Harpercollins.

Northedge, A. (2005) *The Good Study Guide*, 2nd edn. Milton Keynes: Open University Press. (These guides are also available in subject areas such as science and art.)

Shiach, D. (1995) *Basic Grammar*. London: John Murray.

Student finance

You should be able to get a range of student finance guides from government agencies free of charge. For contact details for agencies see How to get further advice (pages 144–151).

Directory of Social Change (2005/6) *Educational Grants Directory 2005/06*. London: Directory of Social Change. (You should be able to find this in a public library or careers centre).

The Grants Register (2005) Basingstoke: Palgrave Macmillan Limited. (You should be able to find this in a public library or careers centre).

Choosing a university

Dudgeon, P. (2005) *The Virgin Alternative Guide to University 2006*. London: Virgin Books.

Heap, B. (2005) *Degree Course Offers: 2006 Entry*. Richmond: Trotman.

Leach, J. (2005) *The Guardian University Guide 2006*. London: Atlantic Books.

O'Leary, J. (2005) *The Times Good University Guide 2006*. London: Times Books.

Trotman (2004) *Mature Students' Directory 2005*. Richmond: Trotman.

Trotman *CRAC Degree Course Guides*. These relate to first degree courses in particular subjects.

Universities and Colleges Admissions Service (UCAS) Guides

UCAS. *Directory 2006 Entry*.

UCAS. *How to Read League Tables*. 2nd edn.

UCAS (2006) *Student Finance Guide.* Kogan Page/UCAS.

UCAS *University and College Entrance: The Official Guide.* Available at public libraries or careers centres.

All UCAS publications can be obtained by contacting the UCAS Distribution Department on 01242 544610. UCAS also publish guides to completing the UCAS application form, guides for mature students and guides for parents.

Student life and survival

Levin, P. (2005) *Excellent Dissertations!* Maidenhead: Open University Press.

Levin, P. (2004) *Sail Through Exams!* Maidenhead: Open University Press.

Levin, P. (2004) *Successful Teamwork!* Maidenhead: Open University Press.

Levin, P. (2004) *Write Great Essays!* Maidenhead: Open University Press.

Moore, S. and Murphy, M. (2005) *How to be a Student: 100 Great Ideas and Practical Habits for Students Everywhere.* Maidenhead: Open University Press.

Race, P. (1998) *How to Get a Good Degree.* Buckingham: Open University Press.

Tracy, E. (2002) *The Student's Guide to Exam Success.* Maidenhead: Open University Press.

BIBLIOGRAPHY

Braid, M. (2005) Women who stick the knife in, *The Sunday Times*, 17 April.

Carlton, S. and Soulsby, J. (1999) *Learning to Grow Older and Bolder*. Leicester: NIACE.

Cassidy, S. (2005) We need more Sam Ryans to encourage women scientists, *Independent*, 11 April.

Hargie, O., Saunders, C. and Dicks, D. (1987) *Social Skills in Interpersonal Communication* 2nd edn. London: Routledge.

Kingston, P. (2005) Lay, Lady, Lay, *Education Guardian*, 3 May.

Leach, J. (2004) *Find it Keep It. The Guardian/NUS Guide to Student Finance*. London: Atlantic Books.

Maxted, P. (1999) *Understanding Barriers to Learning*. London: Campaign for Learning.

Reece, I. and Walker, S. (1997) *Teaching, Training and Learning. A Practical Guide*. 3rd edn. Sunderland. Business Education Publishers Limited.

UCAS (2004) *The Mature Students' Guide to Higher Education*. Cheltenham: UCAS.

UCAS (2004) *The Parent's Guide to Higher Education 2005*. Cheltenham: UCAS and the *Independent*.

INDEX